EAT SMART
IN
INDONESIA

EAT SMART
IN
INDONESIA

How to Decipher the Menu
Know the Market Foods
&
Embark on a Tasting Adventure

Joan and David Peterson

Illustrated by S.V. Medaris

GINKGO PRESS, INC
Madison, Wisconsin

Eat Smart in Indonesia
Joan B. Peterson and David C. Peterson
© 1997 Ginkgo Press, Inc. All rights reserved.

Map lettering is by Gail L. Carlson; color photographs are by John Mimikakis, Joan Peterson, David E. Schrieber and William W. Wongso.

The quote by James A. Michener from "This Great Big Wonderful World," from the March 1956 issue of Travel-Holiday Magazine, © 1956 by James A. Michener, is reprinted by permission of the William Morris Agency, Inc. on behalf of the author.

The recipe for *rendang ayam* is from INDONESIAN REGIONAL COOKING by Sri Owen © 1995 by Sri Owen, reprinted by permission of St. Martin's Press Incorporated.

Library of Congress Catalog Card Number: 97–92899
Publisher's Cataloging in Publication
(Prepared by Quality Books Inc.)
Peterson, Joan (Joan B.)
   Eat smart in Indonesia : how to decipher the menu, know the market foods and embark on a tasting adventure / by Joan & David Peterson.
   p. cm.
   Includes bibliographical references and index.
   ISBN 0-9641168-1-2
   1. Cookery, Indonesian. 2. Indonesia--Guidebooks. 3. Food habits--Indonesia. 4. Diet--Indonesia. I. Peterson, David (David C.) II. Title.
TX4.5.I5P48 1997   641.5'9598
                          QBI97-40220
Printed in the United States of America

To Pak William

His love and knowledge of Indonesian food
added savor to every page

Contents

The Cuisine of Indonesia   1

An historical survey of the development of Indonesian cuisine and the outside influences felt by several millenia of foreign intervention by traders and invaders from many nations.

Regional Indonesian Food   15

A quick tour through the Indonesian islands to see the diversity of cooking styles encountered in traveling the length and breadth of the archipelago.

Tastes of Indonesia   35

A selection of delicious, easy-to-prepare regional and national recipes to try before leaving home.

Shopping in Indonesia's Food Markets   57

Tips to increase your savvy in both the exciting outdoor food markets and modern supermarkets.

Resources   59

A listing of stores carrying hard-to-find Indonesian foods and of groups that focus on travel to Indonesia or offer opportunities for person-to-person contact through home visits to gain a deeper understanding of the country, including its cuisine.

Helpful Phrases   63

Questions in Indonesian, with English translations, which will assist you in finding, ordering and buying foods or ingredients, particularly regional specialties.

Menu Guide   67

An extensive listing of menu entries in Indonesian, with English translations, to make ordering food an easy and immediately rewarding experience.

Foods and Flavors Guide   99

A comprehensive glossary of ingredients, kitchen utensils and cooking methods in Indonesian, with English translations.

Preface

> If you reject the food, ignore the customs, fear the
> religion and avoid the people, you might better
> stay home. You are like a pebble thrown into
> water; you become wet on the surface but you are
> never a part of the water.
> —James A. Michener

As inveterate travelers, we have had many adventures around the world. Except for stints as tour directors for the United Service Organization and the International 4-H Youth Exchange, we have traveled independently, relying on our own research and resources. One way we gauge the success of our trips is how well we become familiar with the native cuisine. To us, there is no more satisfying way to become immersed in a new culture than to mingle with the local people in the places where they enjoy good food and conversation, in their favorite neighborhood cafés, restaurants, picnic spots or outdoor markets. We try to capture the essence of a country through its food, and seek out unfamiliar ingredients and preparations that provide scrumptious new tastes. By meandering on foot or navigating on local buses, we have discovered serendipitously many memorable eating establishments away from more heavily trafficked tourist areas. As unexpected but cherished diners, we have had the pleasure of seeing our efforts in learning the cuisine appreciated by the people in ways that make an understanding of each other's language unimportant.

Each trip energizes us as though it were our first; the preparation for a visit becomes almost as exciting as the trip itself. Once we determine the destination, we begin to accumulate information—buying most, if not all, the current, relevant guide books, raiding the libraries and sifting through our hefty collection of travel articles and clippings for useful data. A high priority for us is the creation of a reference list of the foods, with translations, from the gathered resource materials. For all but a handful of popular European destinations, however, the amount of information devoted to food is limited. General travel guides and phrase books contain only an overview of the cuisine because they cover so many other subjects of interest to travelers. Not surprisingly, the reference lists we have compiled from these sources have been inadequate; too many items on menus were unrecognizable. Of course, some menus have translations but these often are more amusing than helpful, and many waiters cannot provide further assistance in interpreting them. Furthermore, small neighborhood establishments—some of our favorite dining spots—frequently lack printed menus and, instead, post their daily offerings, typically in the native language, on chalkboards outside the door. So unless you are adequately familiar with the language of food, you may pass up good tasting experiences!

To make dining a more satisfying cultural experience for ourselves and for others, we resolved on an earlier vacation that we would improve upon the reference lists we always compiled and research the food "on the spot" throughout our next trip. Upon our return, we would generate a comprehensive guidebook, making it easier for future travelers to know the cuisine. The book that resulted from that "next trip" featured the cuisine of Brazil and represented the first in what would be a series of in-depth explorations of the foods of foreign countries; the second book featured the food of Turkey, and this, the third, covers Indonesia's cuisine. Our intention is to enable the traveler to decipher the menu with confidence and shop or browse in the supermarkets and in the fascinating, lively outdoor food and spice markets with greater knowledge.

Our own journeys have been greatly enhanced because we have sampled unfamiliar foods. One of many illustrations of this in Indonesia occurred in Tuk Tuk, a village along the shore of Lake Toba, North Sumatra. This region is the home of the Batak ethnic group.

American friends visiting Tuk Tuk some months before our arrival had mentioned to a couple running a restaurant that we would be coming to Indonesia to research the cuisine for our guidebook, and the Lake Toba area was on our itinerary. The couple offered to show us how to make a typical Batak dish, the popular *ikan mas panggang,* or grilled goldfish, served with a most interesting sauce called *tinombur,* so we took them up on it when we arrived.

The first step of the learning process involved tagging along with the chef while she bartered for the fish from one of several families who raise them in cages at the edge of the lake. Not confident of our balance on the bamboo scaffolding leading out over the water to the cages, we entrusted the chef to pick out a good one. Bartering was intense but we could tell from her broad smile once it was over that she had gotten a good deal on dinner that night.

Since the cooking of the fish wouldn't be an unusual process—it was grilled—we spent our time watching the preparation of the sauce, *tinombur*. The chef deftly mashed into a paste some fresh roots, spices, chili peppers and tomatoes, using her flat, black stone mortar and a small hand-size oblong stone as a pestle. Candlenuts, used as a binder, had to be sautéed in oil first because they are somewhat toxic when eaten raw. The novel ingredient of the spice paste was called *andaliman,* or *intir intir.* This small, dark green to black berry has a lemony taste, and it imparts a slight numbing sensation to the mouth. Needless to say, the grilled fish with sauce made a memorable meal, but what really intrigued us was *andaliman.* It is a little-known, hardly used spice. The Bataks add it to several dishes, but they may be the only ones who do. We found the scientific name, *Piper ribesioides,* from a Batak/Bahasa Indonesian dictionary; another common name for it, *lada rimba,* translates to jungle pepper. We and several others continue to seek out more information. Perhaps one of our readers will be able to shed some light on this fascinating pepper variety for us.

Everyone confesses both to disliking certain foods and to avoiding others that are unfamiliar. This guide will help steer the traveler away from known problematic foods and will encourage sampling new and unusual ones. The informed traveler will have less concern about mistakenly ordering undesirable food and will, as a result, be more open to experimentation.

The guide has four main chapters. The first provides a history of Indonesian cuisine. It is followed by a chapter with descriptions of regional Indonesian foods. The other main chapters are extensive listings, placed near the end of the book for easy reference. The first is an alphabetical compilation of menu entries, including more general Indonesian fare as well as specialties characteristic of specific islands of the archipelago. Noteworthy, not-to-be-missed dishes with country-wide popularity are labeled "national favorite" in the margin next to the menu entry. Classic regional dishes of Indonesia—also not to be missed—are labeled "regional classic." The second list contains a translation of food items and terms associated with preparing and serving food. This glossary will be useful in interpreting menus since it is impractical to cover in the *Menu Guide* all the flavors or combinations possible for certain dishes.

Also included in the book is a chapter offering hints on browsing and shopping in the food markets and one with phrases that will be useful in restaurants and food markets to learn more about the foods of Indonesia. A chapter is devoted to classic Indonesian recipes. Do take time to experiment with these recipes before departure; it is a wonderful and immediately rewarding way to preview Indonesian food. Most special Indonesian ingredients in these recipes can be obtained in the United States; substitutions for unavailable ingredients are given. Sources for hard-to-find Indonesian ingredients can be found in the *Resources* chapter, which also cites some groups that focus on travel to Indonesia or offer the opportunity to have person-to-person contact through home visits to gain a deeper understanding of the country, including its cuisine.

We call your attention to the form at the end of the book. We would like to hear from you, our readers, about your culinary experiences in Indonesia. Your comments and suggestions will be helpful for future editions of this book. This form can also be used to order additional copies of this book directly from Ginkgo Press, Inc.

selamat jalan dan selamat makan!

JOAN AND DAVID PETERSON
Madison, Wisconsin

Acknowledgments

We gratefully acknowledge those who assisted us in preparing this book. Ciauwindarto Anggara, Irma Nawangwulan, Ellen Rafferty, and William W. Wongso for translations; Beverly and Syamsul Bachri, Bill Dalton, Bapak Gusti Nyoman Darte, Ken Fish, John Hartanto, Wayan Kelepon, Irma Nawangwulan, Winifred Nyhus, Sri Owen, Bernadeth Ratulangi, Gina Rosalina, Dwito Nugroho Satmoko, Tuti Soenardi, Marilyn Staff, Aisyah Sidik Surkatty, Madé Surya, Hayatinufus Afit L. Tobing, Oka Wati and William W. Wongso for contributing recipes from their private collections; S.V. Medaris for her magical illustrations; Gail Carlson for enlivening our maps with her handwriting; Susan Chwae (Ginkgo Press) for a knockout cover design; Lanita Haag (Widen Enterprises) for the excellent four-color separations; Michael Kienitz (DLM Imaging) for the super scans; John Mimikakis for a classy photograph of the authors; and Nicol Knappen (Ekeby) for bringing the text neatly to order.

Thanks also to Ong Hok Ham for providing invaluable assistance on Indonesian history, and to Daisy Hadmoko, Acep Hidayat and especially William W. Wongso, for the encouragement they have given us on this guidebook. Indeed, William W. Wongso should be knighted or otherwise duly recognized for his ongoing herculean efforts to bring Indonesia's delicious cuisine to the attention of the world.

We are indebted to many people for help in identifying regional Indonesian foods and menu items, or providing source material. Thanks to Ciauwindarto Anggara, Dicki Anton, Alice Arndt, Bev and Syamsul Bachri, Gail Carlson, Erin Dickerson, Fred B. Eiseman, Jr., Steven Fortney, Suryatini N. Ganie, Steven Gill, Eka Ginting, Robert Lam, Sandra Hamid-Zilberg, John Hartanto, Barbara Lazewski, Irma Nawangwulan, Leslee Nelson, Philip Nyhus, Sri and Roger Owen, M. Soleh Adi Pramono, Djoko and Asri

Riyanto, David and Janet Schrieber, Karen Schrieber, Jan Siemonsma, Baginda Siregar, Jusman Siswandi, Judy Slattum, Danielle L. Surkatty, Madé Surya, Sisi W. Sutrisno, Hayatinufus Afit L. Tobing, and William W., Lucy and Tia Wongso. Thanks also to Fred B. Eiseman, Jr. and Judy Slattum for the use of unpublished material and Danielle L. Surkatty for illustration materials.

We'd like to thank the following people in Indonesia for presenting cooking demonstrations or introducing us to regional foods: Amna Kusumo (Kafe Solo, Surakarta, Java), Daniel Meury, Chef Dwito Nugroho Satmoko and Ratina Moegiono (Chedi Hotel, Bandung, Java), William W. Wongso (William F & B Management, Jakarta), A. Ning Sudaryatmo (Sarinah Food Court, Jakarta), Agus Sulastiyono, A.A. Daun, Moh. Liga Suryadana, and Suseno Kardigantara (Daun Pisang Restaurant, Bandung, Java), H. Agus I. Montana (Hotel Indra Puri, Bandar Lampung, Sumatra), Ariane Frey, Mok Mok and Chef Ros Manurung (Rumba Homestay and Restaurant, Tuk Tuk, Sumatra), Tilung Lukman (Denai Hotel, Bukittinggi, Sumatra), Dewa Pastika (Keraton Bali Hotel, Jimbaran, Bali), Crescentia Harividyanti (Tugu Hotel, Malang, Java), Wayan Kelepon (Cafe Wayan, Ubud, Bali), Rusiana Hamid and Rita Helivia (Rumah Makan Selera Indonesia, Bandar Lampung, Sumatra), Chef Suardana (Puri Baggis Hotel, Candidasi, Bali), Bapak Gusti Nyoman Darte (Warung CuCu, Campuan-Ubud, Bali), and Agus, Shinta and Roy Wibisono (PT Sarana Wisma Permai, Surabaya, Java).

We are especially grateful to Hayatinufus Afit L. Tobing and William W. Wongso for editing the *Menu Guide* and *Food & Flavors Guide* for accuracy.

Thanks also to Norman and Audrey Stahl, whose unofficial newspaper clipping services kept us well supplied with timely articles about Indonesia, and Dave Nelson for his unflagging encouragement.

And special thanks to Brook Soltvedt, a most perceptive and helpful editor.

EAT SMART

IN

INDONESIA

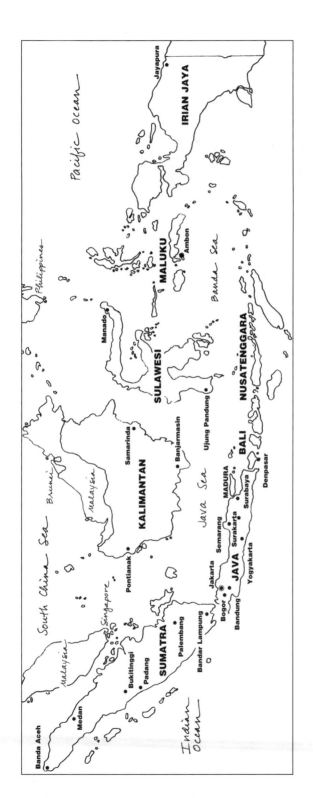

The Indonesian Archipelago

The Cuisine of Indonesia

An Historical Survey

The Indonesian Archipelago, the world's largest, is a vast string of islands straddling the equator in the western Pacific. Over 17,000 islands stretch close to 3,200 miles from the western tip of Sumatra to the eastern edge of Irian Jaya, yet only about 1,000 of them are settled permanently.

The ethnic diversity of the Indonesian people bears witness to several millenia of foreign intervention by traders and invaders from many nations, who were attracted to the islands' riches, especially spices. Indeed, the islands' history reads like an epic of the world's lust for their profusely growing spices. But by the time the outsiders' influences were felt, the Indonesian people were advanced sufficiently to absorb and assimilate other cultural elements into their own traditional political and religious systems. In the process, the Indonesian menu also gained many new entries.

Early History

The earliest people living in the archipelago are believed to have migrated primarily from southern China and Indochina, due to population pressure from the north. Gradual migration, in waves over several millenia, brought the New Stone Age (Neolithic), Bronze and Iron Age cultures.

The Neolithic period, beginning in southeast Asia about 2500 BC, marked the development of permanently settled villages, grain cultivation and animal domestication. Impressions of rice husks and grain found in pottery date the

1

use of rice to at least 2300 BC. Even before this, taro cultivation may have been widespread.

The first permanent farmers primarily worked the richer soil of the archipelago's western islands. Techniques of wet rice agriculture (*sawah* cultivation) were known by 1000 BC. Rice fields were irrigated with water carried in bamboo pipes and were plowed by domesticated buffalos. Oxen, goats, dogs, pigs and chickens were also tamed by this time.

Wet rice cultivation is labor intensive, requiring a complex infrastructure to organize and supervise all aspects of its growth, irrigation and harvest. Early agrarian communities developed an intricate social order to ensure a successful crop of rice, the staple upon which their existence depended. Based on the spiritual and societal obligations of members of these co-operative, rice-growing villages, an elaborate system of unwritten customary law (*adat*) evolved, which regulated all aspects of individual behavior within the towns. This traditional local law persisted and survived frequent challenges to its authority. New religions—Hinduism, Buddhism, Islam and Christianity—would be introduced and embraced, always fitting in with local *adat* law rather than overlying it.

Settlers working in regions unsuitable for wet rice agriculture grew rice by the *ladang* method (dry fields), which required no sophisticated social organization and, consequently, their level of civilization lagged behind that of villages using irrigation.

Menus consisted of fruits, vegetables and roots, among them bananas, breadfruits, yams, taro, coconut and sugar cane, along with fish and the staple rice. Leaves, grasses and barks were also eaten. Meat was a dietary supplement when wild game hunting was good.

The early agrarians were also seafarers. Neolithic boatmen navigated their outrigger boats by the stars as far as Madagascar off the eastern coast of Africa. They were the forerunners of spice traders bearing precious cargoes such as cinnamon and cassia.

By the advent of the Bronze Age, social stratification was well defined, with a clear distinction between rulers and ordinary people. Spiritual life in the form of ancestor worship brought into play elaborate social systems involving religious rites and monuments to commemorate the dead.

Personal possessions buried with the dead chronicled the use of metal (first bronze, then iron) as the primary raw material in the production of utensils and weapons. Of interest are the large bronze kettledrums, highly adorned with figures, made on the mainland of southeast Asia by at least

Quills of cinnamon from an evergreen tree of the laurel family. The inner bark is peeled and rolled, then sun-dried. This spice has been a valuable commodity for thousands of years.

1000 BC and somewhat later, about 500 BC, in Indonesia. Mainland drums were found in specific regions of the Indonesian archipelago along trade routes where commodities such as spices and woods were located. This suggests that drums may have been used for barter and also that foreign trade was widespread in the archipelago before the birth of Christ.

The Chinese

Large ceramic jars of the Han Dynasty have been found in southern Sumatra, western Java and eastern Kalimantan, indicating that regular trading connections between Indonesia and China were established around 200 BC. Sandalwood and other forest products, and nutmeg, mace and cloves were brought back by the early Chinese merchants. One account, perhaps apocryphal, states that Chinese emperors couldn't be addressed by courtiers whose breath hadn't been sweetened first by sucking on cloves.

Some early traders remained in the archipelago, and small groups of artisans and merchants came in the early 1600s following the arrival of the Dutch (see p. 9). The largest influx of Chinese, however, emigrated at the bidding of the Dutch in the latter half of the 1800s, to provide cheap labor for their tin mines in Sumatra and their colonial plantations. Many advanced to entrepreneurial positions while still under Dutch rule. After Indonesia won her independence from the Dutch in 1950, the Chinese remained a dominant force in the business and financial communities.

The Chinese contribution to the diet of the archipelago is very much in evidence today. Tea, noodles, Chinese cabbage, mustard greens, yard-long beans, mung bean sprouts, soybeans and soybean products such as tofu and fermented soybean paste were introduced. Soy sauce is also a culinary gift from the Chinese. The Indonesians sweetened it with palm sugar and formed a thick, syrupy sauce they call *kecap manis,* which is not to be confused with our tomato-based ketchup.

Some of the more common Indonesian dishes are of Chinese origin. These include the popular fried and boiled noodle dishes, *bakmi (mi) goreng* and *bakmi (mi) rebus,* respectively. The classic fried rice, or *nasi goreng,* is also very much a Chinese-inspired dish, as is the small meat- or seafood-filled dumpling (*pangsit*) made with a wonton skin, served in broth. And in most Indonesian kitchens there is a Chinese wok, or *wajan,* to prepare stir-fried dishes.

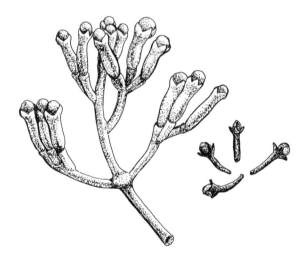

Cloves are the aromatic, unopened flower buds of an evergreen tree once native to a handful of the Indonesian Spice Islands (Malukus). Young green buds, growing in clusters (left), are harvested by hand and spread out on mats to dry in the sun. When dry, the buds become thinner, hard and dark brown (right). Much of today's clove crop is ground and blended with tobacco to make the *kretek* cigarette, which is extremely popular.

The Indians

Trading between India and Indonesia existed by the 1st century AD. Rulers of small coastal kingdoms were introduced to the more civilized, literate and artistic Indian culture by Hindu missionaries accompanying the traders. Eager to gain from the knowledge of the learned scholars and priests (Brahmins), these chieftains included them in their governing bodies and worked to increase missionary migration to their courts.

By about the 2nd century AD, there were several small Hindu–Indonesian kingdoms, primarily in central and western Java, and on the eastern coast of Sumatra. Buddhist concepts were also brought to Indonesia about this time, by the Chinese and Indians, and the first of the foreign religions to impact Indonesia—Hinduism and Buddhism—rapidly gained a foothold.

Indian cultural and religious influences dominated Indonesian society for centuries before being supplanted with Islam. The greatest expression of these concepts was reached in the Buddhist kingdom of Sriwijaya, the maritime empire of southern Sumatra (7th to 13th century) and the agrarian Hindu empire of Majapahit in Java (13th to 14th century).

The Indonesian kitchen was also enriched by the Indian presence. Eggplants, onions and mangoes were introduced, as were aromatic spices such as ginger, coriander, cumin, cardamom and fennel. Present day Indonesian curries (*kare, gulai, gule*) reflect this Indian heritage, but a clear Indonesian stamp is recognizable in these dishes. Regional variations abound, with coconut milk a key ingredient in most of them and chili peppers often providing the main essence.

The Muslims

Islam was introduced to the archipelago as early as 700 AD by Muslim mariners calling at small harbor towns in northern Sumatra, on the Straits of Malacca, an important sea route in southeast Asia. These merchants were Persians and Indians from Gujarat, western India, an area that earlier had been converted to Islam by Persian traders. The first Islamic settlements were established in this coastal region of Sumatra in the 13th century.

An important testimonial to the presence of Muslim communities in northern Sumatra was recorded by the Venetian Marco Polo, who spent five

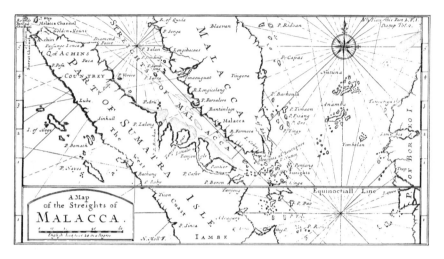

The Straits of Malacca, an 18th-century drawing by Herman Moll, from *Dampier's Voyages,* edited by John Masefield.

months there in 1292. He noted that the kingdom of Perlak, near the present-day city of Langsa, had become Muslim and was called the Sultanate of Pasai. From his accounts we also learn about the culinary habits of the people he encountered there. The staple food was rice, augmented with meat, fish and coconuts, and a beverage made by tapping palm trees. Today's equivalent, *tuak,* is made by extracting the sap of unopened flowers from various types of palm trees, especially the coconut palm. The inhabitants of other kingdoms he visited in Sumatra ate unrecognizable fruits and spices, and made flour from the pith of the sago palm.

The spread of Islam to other port communities along both the east and west coasts of Sumatra, and to other islands of the archipelago by Muslim merchant seamen was slow. Since Hinduism was still the dominant religion in the islands, it was necessary to convince believers that Islam offered something better. After the Malay kingdom of Malacca converted to Islam in 1409, it became a wealthy and prestigious maritime center controlling the trade route from India and Arabia to the west, and China and the Spice Islands (Maluku) to the east. This success hastened the Islamic conversion. By the end of the 15th century, the last of the Hindu–Javanese agrarian kingdoms was won over by the new faith. Islam still is firmly established in the archipelago, with the exception of the island of Bali, whose people practice Hinduism today.

Muslims brought to the Indonesian menu their goat and lamb dishes with richly seasoned yogurt-based sauces. Indonesian cooks adapted these stews to their own taste, and replaced the yogurt with coconut milk. Lamb dishes such as *kambing kurma* are popular in northern Sumatra, the area where Islam first came to Indonesia.

The Portuguese

The first European presence in Indonesia was felt early in the 16th century. Portuguese navigators in search of the fabled Spice Islands (Maluku) and

their bounty of nutmeg, mace and cloves, and Sumatra and Java's precious pepper, captured the profitable Muslim trading empire of Malacca in 1511 and reached the Spice Islands the following year. They quickly gained control of the lucrative trade routes of Asia, and had a near monopoly of the spice trade for a little over 100 years before the Dutch emerged as chief foreign contenders for control of the spice market.

Portuguese missionaries converted only small pockets of the Indonesian population to Christianity. Those arriving later from other European countries similarly had little success with their proselytizing efforts.

The Portuguese brought manioc (cassava) and sweet potatoes to the islands. They had learned how to cultivate manioc and prepare dishes with it from the Tupi Indians in Brazil, a country they discovered in the early 1500s.

Fresh pepper berries, clustered on long spikes. These vine-growers were once worth their weight in gold.

The Spanish

Spain began threatening Portugal's attempted monopoly in the Spice Islands as early as 1521, establishing a trading post on the island of Tidor, a rival of the Portuguese-occupied island of Ternate. The brief Spanish involvement ended in 1529, when King Philip relinquished his claim on the Spice Islands to the Portuguese, turning instead to the Philippine Islands, which had been discovered enroute to Indonesia in 1521. In 1580, Spain was temporarily united with Portugal. The two nations made a concerted but failed effort to slow the decline of Portugal's hold on the spice trade.

The Spanish made several profound contributions to the islands' cuisine. They introduced chili peppers, peanuts, tomatoes and corn, foods they had acquired from South and Central America. The Indonesian palate developed a special fondness for hot chili peppers and peanuts, which quickly became indispensible ingredients in many dishes, condiments and sauces.

The coat of arms with images of cinnamon, cloves and nutmeg, given by Emperor Charles V of Spain to Juan Sebastian de Elcano, upon his return in 1522 from the Spice Islands with a cargo of cloves. Of the five ships Magellan commanded in the first attempt to circumnavigate the globe, Elcano captained the only one to return to Spain.

The English

The English East Indies Company was chartered in the early part of the 17th century to enable the English to compete with the Dutch, whose merchant seamen successfully brought valuable cargoes of spices from Indonesia to Holland a few years earlier. England and Holland signed a treaty providing for peaceful coexistence in their pursuit of spices, but intense rivalry precluded this. Plagued by financial and personnel problems, the English withdrew their effort after about 20 years. Indonesian history records an even briefer English presence 200 years later during the Napoleonic Wars. When the British obtained the Dutch holdings in Indonesia in 1811, Lord Raffles governed in Java for 5 years before power was returned to the Dutch after Napoleon's defeat. The English had little impact on Indonesian cuisine.

The Dutch

The first Dutch spice-seeking voyage to Indonesia took place in 1595, marking the beginning of an almost uninterrupted 350-year tenure in the islands, which profoundly affected the country. In the next 10 years, 12 private expeditions were sent to Indonesia. To eliminate rivalry among Dutch profiteers, the United East Indies Company (VOC) was formed and given autonomy to govern itself.

The Dutch built fortified trading posts throughout the islands, with head-quarters in Batavia (now Jakarta). Their first priority was to establish a monopoly and eliminate competition with rival European traders who had

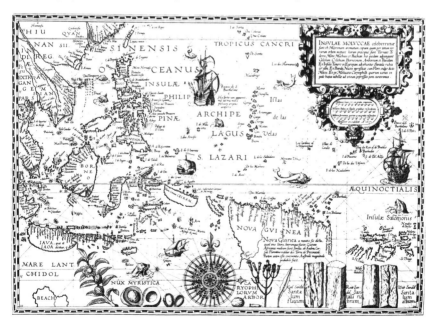

An early Dutch map of the Moluccas (now Malukus), Indonesia's Spice Islands.

made it possible for local rulers to elevate prices. By about the middle of the 17th century, the Dutch had seized the vital trading center of Malacca from the Portuguese and had a monopoly on the clove, nutmeg and mace trade. At the end of the 17th century, they controlled Java and key regions of other islands.

Within a century, however, a variety of factors brought about the decline of the VOC—mismanagement, corruption, the end of the spice monopoly in Asia, by treaty, and changing economic conditions. In 1800, the Dutch trading empire became a colonial empire run by the Netherlands government. Except for a brief period of English rule (1811–1816) and capture by the Japanese in World War II (1942–1945), Indonesia was a Dutch colony. Independence was achieved in 1949 and the Republic of Indonesia proclaimed in 1950.

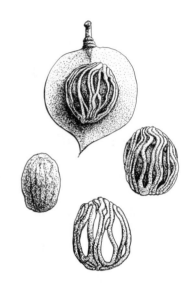

Nutmeg and mace, the spice treasures of the Bandas, a group of islands in the Malukus, or Spice Islands. Top: half a mature nutmeg fruit with its seed (nutmeg) surrounded by mace, the lacy seed covering; right: nutmeg within its shell surrounded by mace; below: mace, and left: nutmeg without its shell.

The Dutch contributed much to the kitchen. In cooler, elevated regions of Indonesia, they grew temperate-climate vegetables from their homeland—carrots, potatoes, turnips, cabbages, red radishes, cauliflower, lettuce and green beans. They brought the coffee plant, introduced the art of brewing beer and left behind a rich legacy of sweet cakes and bread. Layer cakes such as *lapis legit* and *lapis* Surabaya stem from Dutch colonial times.

Special-Occasion Foods

The Islamic calendar has a rich, traditional association with food. The month-long fast, or Puasa (Ramadan), is one of the most important Muslim religious events. The faithful wake by sunrise and fast until sunset. At the break of the daily fast, tea and sweet desserts such as sticky (glutinous) rice cakes are eaten, followed by prayer. Then the joyous, long-awaited fast-breaking meal called *buka puasa* is enjoyed. It typically includes rice and some of the family's favorite foods. *Sahur,* the meal which must be eaten before daybreak, includes rice and leftovers from the meal eaten the evening before.

The feast celebrating the end of Puasa is called Lebaran, or Idul Fitri in Arabic. Typically it is a joyous two-day festival marked by gift giving, gatherings with family and friends, and plenty of snacks and hearty meals. Popular snacks are sticky rice cakes washed down with tea or lemonade.

Throughout the country, the end of the fast is celebrated with dishes such as chicken in a spicy, coconut-milk sauce (*opor ayam*), chicken livers cooked with red chili peppers (*hati ayam sambal goreng*), marbled eggs (*telur pindang*), shrimp crackers (*krupuk udang*) and crisps made from the *melinjo* nut (*emping*). Regional variations of a soup-like dish of mixed vegetables and meat (*soto*) also are eaten. Compressed rice cakes, made in cases woven from coconut fronds (*ketupat*) or in banana leaves (*lontong*), are ubiquitous offerings during the holiday, as are rice cakes cooked in coconut milk and then steamed in banana leaves (*buras*).

Regional dishes augment the national Lebaran menu. For example, in Banjarmasin, South Kalimantan, chicken marinated in a mixture of fresh and dried chili peppers (*ayam masak blabang*) is also eaten at this time. Muslims from northern Sumatra enjoy curried goat (*kare kambing*) and lacy pancakes (*roti jala*). In Padang, western Sumatra, stewed, young jackfruit (*sayur nangka*) and a spicy (hot), sour dish of beef (*pangek daging asam pedas*) are also served. In Palembang, southern Sumatra, curried vegetables (*kare sayur*) and a sweet, steamed cake (*kue lapanjam*) are enjoyed. The Javanese celebrate with beef in coconut sauce (*sambal goreng daging*) and spiced layer cake (*lapis legit*). East Javanese eat curried crabs (*kare kepiting*), while families from Yogyakarta eat marinated chicken (*ayam bacem*).

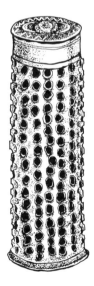

A 17th-century English silver nutmeg grinder drawn from *Spices: The Story of Indonesia's Spice Trade* by Joanna Hall Brierley.

11

Important religious holidays of the Balinese Hindus that are marked by special foods are temple anniversary celebrations called Odalans and festivities called Galungan, which observe the return of deified ancestral spirits to their shrines in family compounds. The five-dish meal associated with these events is called *ebat,* and it is characterized by chopped or pounded ingredients and complex spice mixtures. Traditionally, men prepare these time-consuming specialties.

An *ebat* consists of *lawar,* which has grated coconut, any mixture of meat, vegetables or fruits—one of which must be slivered—and blood; *jejeruk,* turmeric-flavored coconut milk, called *kekalas,* mixed with grated coconut; *urap,* a mixture of grated coconut, vegetables and *kekalas; geguden,* pounded turtle meat mixed with *kekalas* and boiled starfruit leaves; and *serandu,* meat, blood and the coconut residue remaining after squeezing milk from it.

Ritual foods are part of many regional secular ceremonies in Java, called *selamatan,* commemorating life's important transitions such as births, weddings and deaths. These celebrations typically are communal. The traditional dish is *tumpeng,* a conical mound of white rice cooked in coconut milk (*nasi uduk*) or of rice stained yellow with turmeric (*nasi kuning*), which is the centerpiece in a flat, woven basket containing other dishes.

The composition of side dishes is determined by the nature of the holiday. For the important occasion of a child reaching the age of 35 days, at which time the first haircut is given, the cone of rice is surrounded by dishes of beef, chicken and fish, representing foods from creatures that walk, fly and swim,

Ketupat, a container woven of young coconut leaves in which rice is boiled and compressed into a cake traditionally eaten at Lebaran, the end of the Muslim fasting month.

respectively. Another important milestone is the seventh month of pregnancy, the earliest time at which a non-term baby is likely to survive premature birth. Not surprisingly, the theme of the number seven is evident. Six small rice cones surround a seventh, larger one. Seven hard-boiled eggs garnish the customary vegetable dish, *urap,* surrounding the rice cones. Other traditional dishes placed in side trays emphasize seven by having a composition of seven different ingredients or pieces.

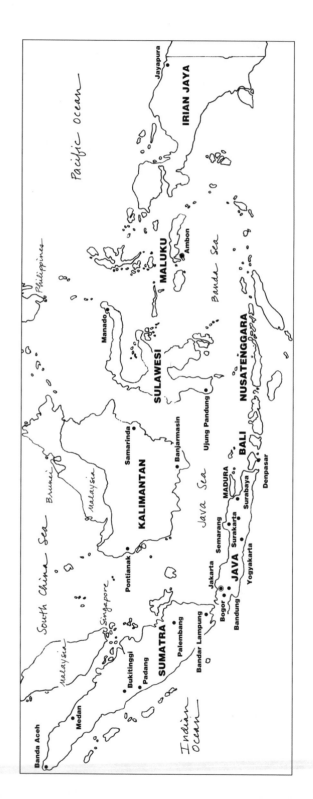

The Indonesian Archipelago

Regional Indonesian Food

A Quick Tour of Indonesian Foods and Their Regional Variations

Indonesian Food in a Nutshell

The delicious cuisine of Indonesia is as clever as it is diverse. Nothing edible in the whole outdoors escapes the cooking pot, and each region puts a twist on traditional cooking processes.

Unfortunately, the historical record of food preparation is sparse. Recipes were passed by word of mouth to succeeding generations and to other regions. Cookbooks were a rarity in 1967 when the Agricultural Department in Jakarta compiled a national cookbook called *Mustikarasa,* or *Crown of Taste,* a large collection of recipes contributed by cooks throughout the archipelago. Literature offered little further insight. According to one of the greatest experts in old Javanese epics, Father P.J. Zoetmulder of the Society of Jesus, the heros in these writings apparently drank a lot, but nothing was written about their meals.

Although the arts in early Javanese courts reached sophisticated levels, the cuisine remained inconsequential, and a gourmet tradition never developed. Today there is a concerted effort by some food authorities to showcase Indonesian cuisine by paying more attention to its presentation and to preserve the culinary heritage by taking measures to slow the proliferation of fast food franchises in the islands.

Unlike typical Western-style dining in courses, Indonesians eat buffet-style, choosing from savory main dishes, condiments and sauces to add to rice. Cooks offer a medley of contrasts, with individual dishes falling into the spicy or mild, hot or cold, crunchy or soft, and sweet or sour categories. In rural settings, prepared food is left on the table for family members to eat when they are hungry rather than for them to dine on together.

15

During colonial times, this meal centered on rice evolved into a gargantuan banquet ritual as the Dutch rulers' need to feel aristocratic was matched by Indonesian hospitality. Diners were served by waiters standing in long lines, each patiently waiting to place a different preparation on the table already overwhelmed by others surrounding the principal dish of rice. The Dutch aptly called this spectacle a *rijsttafel,* or rice table, and despite Indonesia's gaining independence in 1950, it still lives on in some of the islands' upscale hotel restaurants that beguile tourists with a floor show and a "traditional" Indonesian meal.

In general, Indonesian food is characterized by the liberal use of fresh aromatic roots, spices, grasses and leaves for flavor. Mild to hot chili peppers add additional zest. Although the use of chili peppers is common, only certain regional cuisines such as that of the Minangkabau of West Sumatra or the Manadonese of North Sulawesi would be considered really hot. Often-used Indonesian seasonings include fresh ginger root and the ginger-related rhizomes of greater galangal (laos) and lesser galangal. Also common are coriander seeds, cumin, garlic, shallots, cardamom and the bright-orange turmeric root, which flavors and stains food, especially rice, a vivid yellow. Candlenuts function as a binder. Some of the spices for which the world fought in earlier times—nutmeg, mace and cloves—are of marginal use in Indonesian cuisine. Much of the archipelago's clove crop ends up as an additive in Indonesian cigarettes.

Indonesians cook with fresh spices by mashing them to a paste with a flat stone mortar and a small, oblong stone pestle. The paste is sautéed briefly in a little oil to accentuate its fragrance before stock, bruised stalks of lemon grass and flavorful leaves such as Kaffir lime, turmeric and laurel are added to it. A little shrimp paste might be included for enhanced flavor. Toward the end of the cooking process, coconut milk—an essential ingredient in Indonesian cookery—is added. Spicy, coconut milk-based sauces that are simmered until reduced, leave a delicious residue on

Candlenuts (*kemiri*), a flavoring and thickening ingredient in Indonesian cooking. They are cooked and then ground together with fresh spices to make a paste.

foods cooked in them. Sweetness is provided by palm sugar make from the juice (sap) of certain palm trees, especially the coconut and sugar palms. It looks like our brown sugar but has a richer, carmelized taste.

Rice is the all important food on Indonesian menus. Although both regular and sticky (glutinous) rice are grown, table rice is generally of the regular type. Sticky rice is primarily powdered and used to make desserts. There are also red and black varieties of sticky rice, although these are not highly regarded. Black rice is made into a porridge (*bubur hitam*), fermented to produce a slightly alcoholic rice cake (*tape*) tasting like wine, or mixed with white sticky rice and fermented to make wine (*brem*). Red rice ends up on childrens' plates. Note that there are different names for rice, depending on its state. Rice on the stalk is called *padi;* raw, hulled rice is called *beras;* and cooked rice is called *nasi.*

In much of the drier, eastern portion of the archipelago, the terrain and climate are less suitable for rice cultivation, at least for everyday consumption. The main staples here include taro, cassava, corn, potatoes, sweet potatoes and sago. All are cooked in many ways, according to local custom, including the ingenious method of roasting in sections of green bamboo over a fire.

Not surprisingly, most dietary protein comes from fish. Tuna, mackerel, and red snapper are favorites from the ocean. Popular freshwater fish are milkfish, carp and knifefish. Dishes range in complexity from grilled fish (*ikan bakar*) to the labor-intensive preparation of stuffed milkfish (*bandeng isi*). To make it, the flesh, bones and all, is extracted through the gills while making every effort not to tear the skin. After a spicy stuffing of deboned, cooked flesh is reinserted through the gills, the fish is steamed and baked.

Among seafood, shrimp is one of the most versatile and popular. A condiment (*petis*) is made from jellied shrimp shells and a more pungent one (*trasi*) from fermented shrimp. Just a bit of these can heighten the flavor of a dish.

In the meat and poultry category, chicken is the obvious favorite. Since they are free-running, their meat requires tenderizing by boiling before further cooking. An especially fussy and innovative treatment of chicken (*ayam kodok*) involves creating a frog-shaped structure out of an emptied, intact chicken skin once it has been re-filled with stuffing made from the removed meat, and sewn shut. After the desired shape is achieved with gentle flattening. the "chicken" is steamed and roasted until crispy. Although the Balinese and ethnic Chinese eat duck, its eggs are more

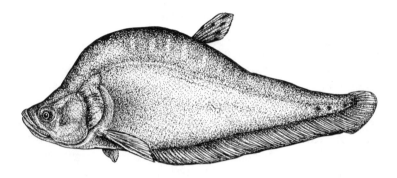

Ikan belida, or knifefish, a flat, eel-like fish popular in the southern region of Sumatra. Its flesh is mixed with sago flour to create a paste central to many popular dishes.

universally eaten than the meat. Meat from cattle and buffalo is consumed by the nation's Muslim and Christian populations. Cattle aren't extensively raised in Indonesia, however, so a dish of beef probably contains buffalo meat. This would explain the lack of a dairy food tradition, although milk and cheese are available in some supermarkets. Goat, also enjoyed, is a prominent item on Muslim holiday menus. The word for goat (*kambing*) also means sheep, but the islands' climate is too hot to raise sheep to any extent. Pork is a specialty of non-Muslim Indonesians. Bali's spit-roasted suckling pig (*babi guling*) is famous. The version made in North Sulawesi, (*babi putar*), is not as well known. The classic Indonesian treatment of meat, and offal, too, is *sate*—small pieces of meat are marinated, threaded on thin bamboo skewers and grilled. Some versions call for minced meat which has to be wrapped around thicker skewers.

Both temperate and tropical vegetables gleam in the markets. A good sampler of some less-common ones is *lalap,* an often enjoyed raw vegetable salad, each of whose ingredients is said to cure a specific body ailment. Several leafy, aquatic plants similar in flavor to our spinach are used in soup-like vegetable dishes (*sayur*). Even the edible leaves from many fruit and vegetable plants—papaya, mango, starfruit, manioc (cassava), yard-long bean, sweet potato and taro, to name a few—are eaten as vegetables, raw or cooked. So lush is the vegetation that much of the edible foliage growing in Indonesia can be had simply for the picking. Soybeans, an important, inexpensive source of protein, are eaten in the form of tofu or as tempe, a cake of cooked soybeans mixed with a mold and fermented in banana leaves for a few days.

Indonesia's tropical fruits are a wondrous assortment of familiar and unknown types. One of the most highly prized is the mangosteen, a purple fruit about the size of a lime, with scrumptious, white segmented flesh. The exotic, hairy-skinned *rambutan* has highly regarded tart, translucent white flesh. A new experience for most is the taste of the much maligned *durian*, whose fetid aroma keeps all but the very adventuresome from trying its interesting custard-like flesh. Some fruits are candied by boiling in sugar syrup. A favorite (*manisan pala*) is made from the flesh of the nutmeg fruit. A fruit snack with universal appeal is a mixture of raw, unripe (tart) fruits topped with *rujak*, a spicy, sweet sauce. Fruits with very tart skin or flesh are used as souring agents. Strolling through fruit markets is always enjoyable, but it is particularly so in Bali, where fruit sellers display their wares so attractively, piling each basketful in tall, perfect mounds.

The traditional Indonesian diet has no soft, leavened bread. Instead, crisp crackers (*krupuk*) accompany meals. They are made of several types of flour and are flavored primarily with fish or shrimp. Similar chips made from kernels of the *melinjo* nut are called *emping*.

Appetizers include several kinds of fritters (*rempah* and *perkedel*) made with chopped ingredients blended together and deep-fried. Standard combinations are meat with corn or boiled potatoes, and meat with coconut. Crisp savory wafers made with peanuts (*rempeyek*), and thin, folded crepes (*martabak*) with savory or sweet fillings, are other delicious choices.

Indonesian soups come in two varieties; both are hearty one-dish meals of meat and vegetables. A *soto* has rich, seasoned broth while a *sop* has clear, mildly seasoned broth. Incredibly, the broth of *sop kambing*, a soup featuring goat, contains a most unexpected addition—cow's milk!

Condiments and sauces round out the Indonesian menu. Meals have at least one condiment, and all have some chili peppers and a number of key ingredients such as tomatoes, shallots, garlic, shrimp paste and soy sauce, Indonesia's beloved seasoning, usually sweetened with palm sugar. A family of pickled relishes (*acar*) contains cucumbers and other vegetables, especially carrots, in a sweet and sour sauce. The versatile peanut is the basis for the best known of Indonesian sauces. It is a salad and vegetable topping and a favorite dipping sauce for *sate*.

Dessert platters most often contain fresh fruit. Bananas are clear favorites along with the revered *durian*. Sweets are enjoyed socially with tea or coffee. Sticky (glutinous) rice flour is featured in many of them, along with coconut milk, grated coconut and palm sugar. It is hard to resist *kelepon*, bite-size balls of boiled rice-flour dough filled with palm sugar and covered with grated coconut.

Indonesians usually drink tea, either iced or hot, with their meals. Since the population is largely Muslim, alcoholic beverages are not served as a rule. Many creative, colorful drinks made with flavored syrup, coconut milk and fruit are enjoyed in addition to tea and coffee. Palm sugar and bits of colored rice-flour dough are delicious additions to these concoctions. A great tasting beverage is *es alpokat,* a smooth shake made with the unusual combination of avocado and chocolate. Another thirst quencher is *es selasih,* an iced drink made of mixed fruit and coconut water, with the uniquely flavorful addition of dried basil seeds that have been swollen in hot water, causing their surface to become gelatinous.

Fresh juice or sap *(tuak manis)* from unopened palm tree flowers, especially from the coconut palm, is also a refreshing beverage. Within a day, however, fermentation is well on its way and a yeasty, beer-like alcoholic toddy is produced *(tuak wayah)*. Distillation of *tuak* produces a strong brandy-like drink called *arak.*

One can sample the foods of Indonesia in diverse settings. The simplest eateries are small food stalls providing stand-up service, and vendors' push-carts. The latter are called *kaki lima,* or "five-legged food vendor," to describe the two-footed vendor and his two-wheeled cart with a small-wheeled stand in the back to rest the cart. Both offer at most one or two items. Modest, sit-down places *(warung)* are semi-permanent "lean-tos." The

The mangosteen *(manggis)*, one of nature's most exquisite fruits, must not be missed in Indonesia. Beneath the thick purple rind is delicious, white, segmented flesh.

menu in Indonesian is written prominently on an awning that also serves as a privacy screen. Cooks offer a handful of inexpensive, authentic Indonesian specialties, which are eaten while sitting on benches at a long table shared with other diners, or even on rugs on the floor. Snacks and other specialty tidbits are arranged at the center of the table and invariably prompt impulse buys. Streets everywhere are lined with these popular, makeshift dining spots, and some of them have established quite a reputation for excellence in their specialties. Those selling just coffee cater to male patrons only. A *rumah makan* has permanent walls and, as a rule, a more elaborate choice of authentic dishes. Menus, if available, will be in Indonesian. *Restoran* is the name used by establishments catering primarily to the tourist trade, and as such, they provide Westernized Indonesian food and menus in English. Chinese-run restaurants usually also use the name *restoran*. Remember, however, that eatery classifications can be somewhat arbitrary.

The Greater Sundas: Sumatra, Java and Kalimantan

Three of the archipelago's five major islands, Sumatra, Java and Kalimantan, comprise the Greater Sunda group. They, and several in between, lie on the Sunda continental shelf.

Sumatra

Sumatra is the western end of the immense Indonesian archipelago. Its rich volcanic soil and tropical wet climate support lush tropical vegetation. Diverse ethnic groups, predominantly Muslim, make up the population, which is second only to Java in size.

Many exciting cuisines will be encountered in Sumatra. Indian and Arabic influences accentuate the foods of the provinces of Aceh and North Sumatra. Examples are curried goat dishes, especially *gulai bagar* and *gulai kambing.* The sauces, however, will be tempered with Sumatran additions of coconut milk and chili peppers, and bear less resemblance to the flavors generally associated with Indian curries. For those who like brains, *gulai otak* is a classic. Lacy pancakes (*roti jala*) made by drizzling thin streams of batter into a heated frying pan traditionally accompany curries.

Sumatra's largest city, Medan, is in North Sumatra. Local menu specialties are *soto* Medan, a chicken or beef soup in coconut-based broth, served with a potato croquette, and *gulai ikan kakap,* curried snapper.

A basketful of *krupuk*, crisp crackers made of several types of flour flavored mainly with fish or shrimp. They are eaten as snacks or with meals. Indonesians have no soft, leavened bread in their traditional diet.

A simple but scrumptious treat served in a banana leaf is *putu buluh*. Rice and palm sugar are steamed in a small section of bamboo, then popped out and topped with grated coconut. *Dodol,* a soft fudge made of sticky (glutinous) rice, coconut milk and palm sugar, is Perbaungan's specialty.

North Sumatra is also the home of the Christian Batak ethnic group, many of whom live in the vicinity of Lake Toba. Some raise golden carp (*ikan mas*), and cages of these colorful goldfish are easy to spot at lake's edge. Some chefs let you choose a fish, which they then roast to perfection (*ikan mas panggang*) and serve with *tinombur,* a condiment containing the exotic spice called jungle pepper (*lada rimba* and *andaliman*). The lemony-tasting berries impart a slight numbing sensation to the lips and mouth. Not much is known about this pepper species; the Batak may be the only people savoring its flavor. They use it in several dishes, including a ceremonial preparation (*arsik*) of fried golden carp stuffed with bamboo shoots or with yard-long beans. Pork is a favorite meat of the Batak people. They offer *piong duku babi,* minced pork and chopped manioc (cassava) leaves in coconut milk, cooked in green bamboo sections. The Karonese, a group of Batak people living near the North Sumatran city of Berastagi serve *babi panggang,* roast pork with rice. These Batak pork dishes usually include pork blood.

The Muslim Minangkabau people in West Sumatra province are renowned for their spicy food laced with fiery chili peppers, a cuisine most frequently called Padang-style after the name of the provincial capital,

Padang. Restaurants serving these Minangkabau specialties exist throughout much of the archipelago, and all display and serve them in the same flamboyant style. Large round basins containing mounds of each dish are arranged in the window in several rows, one on top of each other, to tempt the hungry. Diners have no need to order because a waiter brings a sampler of everything available. He arrives with miniature platesful, all balanced on one arm, and deftly puts them on the table. One only pays for the food one eats from the selection offered. Apparently sampling the sauces in otherwise untouched dishes doesn't increase the tab.

Perhaps the best known dish in the Minangkabau repertoire is *rendang*. Pieces of meat undergo prolonged simmering in a rich, spicy coconut-based sauce, until the water evaporates and the coconut milk turns to oil. The meat becomes coated with a darkened residue of spices. Food cooked this way remains unspoiled for a long time without refrigeration and is typical road food for travelers. The dish is called *kalio* if the meat is cooked until the sauce is only partially reduced. The local version of *sate* is *sate* Padang, and it consists of marinated chunks of tripe, tongue, kidneys and heart, served with a spicy dipping sauce. A festive wedding preparation is *singgang ayam,* spread-eagled chicken cooked in coconut milk and spices and then roasted until crispy.

Minangkabau food is fun to discover in Bukittinggi, a charming university town encircled by mountains. Many novel items, such as yogurt cultured from buffalo milk in green bamboo sections, will be found in its split-level outdoor market. The milk curdles as a result of a naturally occurring culture within the bamboo. This milk product is the basis for a popular local treat (*ampiang dadiah*) containing palm sugar, grated coconut and sticky (glutinous) rice that has been fried, flattened and dried. Other regional dishes are *ayam balado*, browned chicken in hot chili pepper sauce, *dendeng balado,* spicy, sun-dried meat, and *pangek ayam* Padang, yard-long beans and fried chicken in spicy coconut milk. The Bukittinggi market usually offers a super treat from the nearby village of Kapau. Women prepare a spread that has come to be known as *nasi* Kapau—rice served with a selection of meat and vegetable dishes flavored with tamarind, turmeric and hot chili peppers in the fashion of these villagers. Big porcelain basins contain meat, fish and vegetable dishes, including a favorite curry (*gulai kacang panjang*) of uncut yard-long beans. Quite novel and delicious is *paruik,* a sausage stuffed with a mixture of seasoned, beaten duck eggs. The sausages are simmered in spicy coconut milk until the milk turns to oil and the spices coat the sausage.

The specialty of Palembang, South Sumatra, is a versatile paste of sago flour and mashed flesh of the popular local knifefish (*ikan belida*). This paste is the raw material for several regional specialties. In *empek empek,* it is formed into a cake and served on cellophane noodles, covered with sweet-sour sauce. With a hard-boiled egg tucked inside the cake, the dish becomes *kapal selam.* Two soups have balls made of the paste; *model* contains the balls, tofu

A skewer-less *sate* made with a mixture of minced knifefish (*ikan belida*) and sago flour, steamed in a banana leaf.

and cucumber, *tekwan* just the balls. The area's version of *sate* uses this fish paste, but the mixture is steamed in banana leaves, not wrapped onto skewers and grilled.

A specialty of Bandar Lampung in Lampung province at the southern tip of Sumatra is *baung pindang,* a dish of local catfish (*baung*) simmered in spicy and sour water-based broth. *Gabus,* a freshwater snakehead fish will also be available. Other local dishes are *sayur asam,* a sour soup-like preparation of mixed vegetables with the young nuts and leaves of the *melinjo* tree, flavored with tamarind and fermented fish paste, and a dessert called *kolak pisang,* a sweet compote made with bananas stewed in coconut milk and palm sugar flavored with leaves called *daun pandan.*

Java

Java is home to nearly two-thirds of the archipelago's inhabitants. Its rural population is the densest in the world. Farmers work fertile plots of rich volcanic soil flanking the island's central mountainous region. Sugar, rice, tea and tobacco are major crops.

Indonesia's capital, Jakarta, is an administratively autonomous region on the northwestern coast of the island, with over 10 million people of numerous ethnic groups. This sprawling cosmopolitan city is awesome to visit despite its noise and traffic. Local specialties are *ketoprak,* a bean sprout, tofu and rice noodle salad flavored with sweet soy sauce, and topped with sweet-sour peanut sauce, and *nasi uduk,* a combination platter of rice cooked in coconut milk and topped with crispy, fried shallots, served in a banana leaf, plus several fried foods along with *pepes,* a tofu- or anchovy-based mixture steamed in banana leaves. Other foods associated with Jakarta are *bakmi goreng (mi goreng),* stir-fried egg noodles with bits of vegetables and sometimes meat or shrimp, and *gado gado,* a salad of blanched or steamed vegetables topped with a sauce made with spices and ground peanuts. *Soto* Betawi is a beef soup with meat, tripe, offal and potatoes. It is a dish originating with the Betawi ethnic group indigenous to Jakarta.

The predominantly Muslim island is divided into West, Central and East Java provinces. Each province has, of course, a multitude of local food specialties, but a general classification accords the Central Javanese with an insatiable sweet tooth, the West Javanese with a preference for sour tastes, and the East Javanese choosing a middle ground, and especially enjoying the flavor fish pastes impart to foods.

The province of West Java, historically known as Sunda, is the home of the Sundanese people. It is fairly mountainous and agricultural. Those who visit the area make a point to see the charming city of Bogor, with its famous botanical gardens in the foothills near Jakarta, and the provincial capital of Bandung, with its magnificent views, undulating tea plantations and cooler climate at 2,400 feet above sea level. Two regional specialties of Bogor include *laksa* and *karedok. Laksa* is a soup-like dish of rice noodles, chicken, hard-boiled eggs, and bean sprouts flavored with ginger and turmeric in chicken broth and coconut milk. *Karedok* is a special salad made with fresh raw vegetables, served with peanut sauce and strongly flavored *kencur,* or lesser galangal, a pungent rhizome of the ginger family. Another local dish is *asinan,* a mixture of fresh, crunchy fruits and vegetables in a hot (spicy) sweet and sour sauce containing peanuts.

Bandung specialties are *bakso tahu goreng,* fried tofu stuffed with meat paste and topped with peanut sauce; *mi kocok,* soup with egg noodles, beef knuckle, leeks, chili peppers and blanched bean sprouts; and *soto* Bandung, beef soup with fried soybeans, daikon radish and lemon grass in clear broth.

Other West Javanese specialties are *bajigur,* a hot drink made of coconut milk, coffee and spices; *bandrek,* a hot drink made with coconut milk, grated coconut, ginger, palm sugar and black pepper. The city of Cianjur, whose long-grain rice crop is highly prized, serves *gepok pukul* Cianjur, cooked beef, pounded and shredded, then fried and tied together with bamboo. *Ikan salai,* smoked fish, is a specialty of Pekanbaru. *Nasi langgi,* rice with dried beef, an omelette and shrimp sauce, and *nasi lengko,* rice with goat meat grilled on skewers and served with tempe, tofu, cucumber, bean sprouts and peanut sauce are specialties of Cirebon. Cirebon's famous *sate* is *sate kalong,* pieces of beef pounded very flat and grilled on skewers. The meat is flavored with a sweet spice mixture and served with a special sauce. Vendors begin selling it in the early afternoon when the fruit bats (*kalong*) also make their appearance. Also associated with Cirebon is *sayur lodeh,* mixed vegetables blanched in coconut milk and flavored with the leaves and nuts (outer skin) of the *melinjo* tree.

Central Java is the primary tourist destination on the island. Major attractions include ancient structures such as the 9th century Hindu temple complex at Prambanan, and Borobudur, the massive 8th century Buddhist masterpiece, the largest temple built by these people in the world. Both are within comfortable driving distance from Yogyakarta, a city of classic culture, which still operates as a self-governing sultanate, an administratively separate province within Central Java.

The most famous dish of Yogyajakarta is *gudeg,* a combination plate of unripe jackfruit cooked in coconut milk, a chicken dish (*opor ayam*) cooked in spicy, coconut-based sauce lacking chili peppers, rice, a piece of buffalo skin that has been processed into a cracker snack and a dollop of coconut cream sauce. Interesting sweetmeats are *bakpia,* dough filled with a mixture of mung beans and cane sugar, and *geplak,* a sweet cake made of sticky (glutinous) rice, cane sugar and grated coconut formed into different shapes.

Specialties of the provincial capital of Semarang are *gimbal tahu* Semarang, chunks of tofu deep-fried in tempura-like batter and served with

A *warung* specializing in oxtail soup (*sop buntut*) in Solo (Surakarta), Central Java.

sweet soy sauce, spring rolls (*lumpia*) and a puffy, fried yeast doughnut called *bolang baling*. A molded butter cake (*pukis* Banyumas) is a specialty of Banyumas, as is a thin fermented soybean cake (*tempe mendoan*) individually wrapped in a banana leaf. *Soto* Pekalongan, a beef and vegetable soup with tripe and fermented soybean paste is a specialty of Pekalongan. Tegal's special soup is beef with vegetables, tripe and cellophane noodles. Tegal is also known for its tea (*teh poci* Tegal) made of jasmine tea and rock sugar brewed in a clay pot. *Sate kelinci* is a local treat in the city of Tawangmangu. It features rabbit meat. *Ayam goreng* Kalasan, chicken simmered in coconut water and then deep-fried, is a speciality of Kalasan. It is also called *ayam* mBok Berek after mBok (Mrs.) Berek, who created the dish, having discovered the tenderizing effect of the coconut water on the meat.

Another destination for visitors to Central Java is Surakarta, commonly called Solo, the captivating sister city of Yogyakarta, and itself an important cultural center. *Gampol plered,* a sweet snack made with rice flour, coconut milk and spices, is a specialty of the area, as is *nasi liwet,* a combination plate of boiled rice served with chicken, giblets, pear-shaped chayote squash cooked in thick coconut milk, and beef skin crackers. The local *sate* (*sate buntel*) is balls of minced lamb and onion wrapped in caul. Also popular as a macho drink is *susu segar madu telur,* often written SMT, a mixture of fresh milk, honey and beaten eggs. It is touted as an invigorating drink to enhance virility and health.

Of Java's three provinces, East Java is least visited. Its biggest draw is Mt. Bromo, an active, smoking volcano, with spectacular views of the countryside for those who trek to the peak and await sunrise. But there is much to see and eat in this rather neglected region of the island, with its fields of rice, sugar cane, tea and coffee. The province also includes the island of Madura.

Surabaya, the highly industrialized provincial capital of East Java, is the second largest city of Indonesia. Tiny shellfish called *kupang* are local to the area and are served in a rich broth containing cubes of compressed rice. The local *sate* is *sate kerang*, clams grilled on bamboo skewers. A treat that may take some seeking is *semanggi,* chunks of potatoes, boiled bean sprouts and the steamed leaves of a small aquatic variety of clover, topped with a spicy sauce of mashed sweet potatoes and fermented fish or shrimp paste. It is served in a banana leaf and eaten with rice crackers.

A dessert specialty of Surabaya and Madura is *bubur cenil,* served in a banana leaf. It contains coconut milk, beads and chunks of colored sago-flour dough and bits of cake made with rice flour, topped with palm sugar.

Another dessert specialty is *lapis* Surabaya, a three-layer cake make with two vanilla layers separated by a chocolate one, with jam between each layer.

Nearby Malang is a charming, elevated city in the heart of a prosperous area growing vegetables and fruits, especially apples. A specialty of Malang called *arem arem* contains tempe, bean sprouts and chunks of compressed, sticky (glutinous) rice. It is covered with sweet soy sauce and coconut water, and topped with chopped peanuts and grated coconut. An intriguing dessert is *angsli,* a warm dessert made of coconut milk, bread cubes, roasted peanuts, colorful bits of dried tapioca and small squares of cake formed from extruded sticky rice-flour dough. Another local specialty is *nasi empok,* a dish of rice mixed with corn flour.

Lamongan's featured soup is *soto ayam* Lamongan, chicken soup made with shrimp stock and topped with fried garlic or chopped cashews. A soup associated with the island of Madura is *soto* Madura, beef soup with meat, tripe and tail. A tasty sweet from the town of Babat near Surabaya is *wiengko* Babat, giant, glutinous, coconut pancakes. A specialty of the town of Kertosono is *soto* Kertosono, beef ribs stewed in a spicy coconut-based sauce containing cloves. Other specialties of the province are *kilkil,* a rich stew made with goat and cow's hocks, and *rawon,* a spicy meat stew flavored and colored black with *kluwek,* the nut of the *kepayang* tree.

Kalimantan

Roughly three-fourths of the island originally known as Borneo, Kalimantan is a huge and underpopulated region of Indonesia. The Sultanate of Brunei and the Malaysian states of Sabah and Sarawak comprise the rest of the island. Kalimantan is divided into four provinces: West, South, Central and East Kalimantan. Much of the land is roadless jungle, and most of the people live in villages along waterways or in coastal cities. Tourists visiting this island are primarily interested in exotic wildlife, conservation and the indigenous inland tribes of Central Kalimantan.

Indonesia began an extensive transmigration program in the late 1960s to eliminate overcrowding, providing plots of land and housing to families willing to relocate to frontier settlements in Kalimantan and elsewhere. The principal groups now living in Kalimantan are ethnic Chinese, indigenous tribes and Indonesians from other islands in the archipelago, especially many relocated farmers from overpopulated Java, Madura, Bali and Lombok. Not unexpectedly, many dishes of the area were brought from other islands.

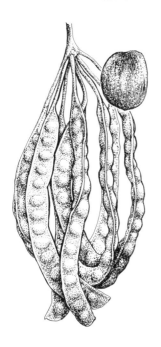

Pete, foot-long pods of a tree-grown broad bean. Young pods are eaten as a vegetable, sliced and fried. Skinned beans are especially popular as a fried snack.

Menu highlights from Kalimantan include *amplang kuku macan,* crescent-shaped snacks flavored with fish, and *jangan asam daging,* a sour vegetable soup with meat. Banjarese food perhaps best typifies the island's offerings. In South Kalimantan's provincial capital of Banjarmasin, look for *masak hijau,* spicy (hot) chicken with green chili peppers and tomatoes, *ikan asam pedas* Banjar, a sour-hot (spicy) preparation of fish, and *soto* Banjar, chicken broth with cellophane noodles and hard-boiled duck eggs, which is served with potato fritters and chunks of compressed rice steamed in small cases woven of coconut palm fronds. Also offered is *itik panggang* Banjar, roast duck; *buah jingah,* sweet-potato fritters and a small freshwater fish called *ikan saluangan.*

Sulawesi

Near the center of the archipelago is the large island of Sulawesi (formerly Celebes) with its extraordinary configuration of four peninsulas jutting from a central, mountainous core, each a separate province. Tourism is focussed in the southwestern and northern peninsulas.

The Christian Minahasans predominate in North Sulawesi. They are blessed with rich volcanic soil and grow crops of corn, coffee, nutmeg, cloves and coconut for *copra,* the dried coconut meat from which cooking oil is extracted. The port city of Manado, the provincial capital, and nearby Tomohon, with its bustling market, are good locations to explore the local cuisine.

In the kitchen, Minahasans are renowned for their heavy hand with hot chili peppers. Dishes including the words *rica rica* mean they are cooked with a super-hot spice paste containing red chili peppers, shallots, ginger and lime juice. An example would be *ikan rica rica,* fish cooked in this nippy sauce. Food is often slow-cooked in freshly cut bamboo sections, a cooking style shared by several Indonesian groups, including Sumatrans and the inland tribes (Dayak) of Kalimantan.

Local specialities are *asam masak di bulu,* chicken cooked in green bamboo sections, *ayam tuturuga,* curried chicken, *tai kuda,* sweet-potato fritters, and *bubur* Manado, a bright-yellow porridge made of corn, manioc (cassava), pumpkin, spinach and rice, seasoned with fish paste and chili peppers. It is also known as *tinutuan.* A dessert treat is *gemblong,* a crunchy fried ball of sticky (glutinous) rice carmelized with palm sugar. A popular salad (*gohu*) of unripe papaya in fermented bonito fish sauce, called *bakasang,* and lime. *Panada* is a popular pasty filled with smoked tuna. *Cakalang fufu,* or smoked tuna, is an important staple. *Saksang* is roast pig cooked with pork blood, which is also a specialty of the Batak in North Sumatra. *Sate* Manado is made with marinated pork. Other local offerings are *ayam bakar rica,* grilled chicken with hot peppers, and *lalampa,* a small cake make with sticky (glutinous) rice cooked in coconut milk and filled with a smoked tuna mixture. It is grilled in a banana leaf. Rice cooked in green bamboo sections lined with young banana leaves is called *nasi jaha.* Exotic menu items for the adventurous include *keluang,* a large fruit-eating bat called a flying fox, and *peret,* the fruit rat, which has a white-tipped tail.

The Muslim Buginese and Makassarese people inhabit the southwest peninsula (South Sulawesi). Major crops are irrigated rice, coffee, corn, sugar cane and tobacco. Large grazing areas permit cattle raising. The provincial capital is Ujung Pandang (formerly Makassar). Regional specialties are *ikan woku,* fish rubbed with a paste of candlenuts, ginger and chili peppers mixed with chopped tomato, turmeric, mint and green onion, then wrapped in a banana leaf and grilled, *ayam woku*, a casserole of chicken cooked in a paste of chili peppers,

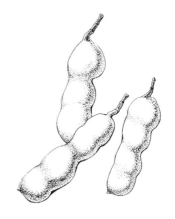

Pods of tamarind (*asam*) containing seeds surrounded by tart, sticky, red-brown pulp used as a souring agent.

ginger, garlic and shallots mixed with chopped leeks, *coto* (*soto*) Makassar *campur*, beef tripe soup, *coto* (*soto*) Makassar *daging,* a meaty soup-like dish with broth mixed with a spice paste and freshly ground peanuts. It traditionally is served with a rice cake called *buras*. A delicious local treat is *es pallubutung,* made with bananas in a thick, creamy sauce containing coconut and rice. Also on local menus are *kare ayam* Makassar, chicken curry with lemon grass and laos, *nasi kabuli,* a dish of Arabic origin with rice and fried lamb or chicken with curry sauce, and *pulu mara,* boiled fish in savory sauce. A popular local favorite is *ikan baronang bakar,* or grilled *baronang,* a large seawater fish prized in South Sulawesi.

The Torajans also inhabit the southwest peninsula, living somewhat isolated in a fertile highland plateau in an area called Tanatoraja, land of the Torajan people. The city of Rantepao is the major tourist center from which treks are made to the region's attractions and ritualistic religious rites.

The Torajans grow rice, vegetables, particularly sweet potatoes, and coffee. Foods are commonly slow-cooked in bamboo sections. This cooking style is called *pa'piong* (*pakpiung*). White sticky (glutinous) rice with coconut milk, and many chicken, pork or fish dishes are prepared this way. For example, *ayam dibulu* is a dish of chicken, bones and all, cooked in spices within the bamboo section.

Bali

Beautiful and exotic Bali is peerless—a tiny island separated from Java by little more than a mile, and the last of the Hindu enclaves in the archipelago. Despite the enormous popularity of Bali as a tourist destination, much of the island still is untouched. Its many volcanoes form the island's backbone and have, over the millenia, left rich soil, which supports coffee and clove plantations in the cool plateaus in the highlands and countless manicured rice terraces meandering down mountain slopes.

Balinese cooking is hot and spicy, and is characterized by the use of special spice pastes (*bumbu*) to flavor particular dishes according to tradition. Balinese *sates* are primarily made with minced, rather than cubed meat, which is wrapped like drumsticks around thick skewers, often parts of the stalk of ginger plants. Four general types are available. *Sate* Bali *asam* is a piquant paste of minced, spiced pork; *sate* Bali *empol* is a paste of chopped meat, spices and coconut milk; *sate* Bali *kebelet* is a paste of liver covered by a paste of chopped meat mixed with spices and coconut; and *sate* Bali *limbat* is a paste of chopped meat, spices and grated coconut. The Balinese love duck and have a classic dish made with it, sometimes, however, substituting chicken. *Bebek betutu* is a dish of whole, dressed duck stuffed with a spice paste, and grilled or slow-cooked underground in hot embers. When cooked underground, the duck is wrapped in palm leaves, covered with rice hulls and placed inside a ceramic bowl. *Jukut urap* is the Balinese version of a popular steamed vegetable salad (*urap*) enjoyed elsewhere in the archipelago. The Balinese version is a mixture of blanched, chopped vegetables, especially string beans and starfruit

Betanten, a tall, ornate food offering borne to the temples on the heads of Balinese women. They contain many artfully arranged foods, even on occasion a whole roasted duck.

leaves, mixed with spices and grated coconut. *Lawar* is one of the ceremonial dishes included in large feasts. It contains any of several combinations of minced meat and finely chopped (slivered) vegetables, leaves, spices and fruits. The name of each *lawar* indicates its key ingredient. If the traditional ingredient of fresh blood is not desired, a *lawar putih* can be requested. *Serombotan* is a salad of raw and cooked vegetables topped with spicy, grated coconut. *Tum hati ayam* is a dish of minced chicken liver mixed with spices and grated coconut, and steamed in a banana leaf. Young shoots of banana plants are eaten as a vegetable, often boiled in duck stock. *Sayur ares* is a sour soup-like dish of boiled young banana tree stems.

Nusatenggara

The Nusatenggara (southeasterly islands) are a chain of about 600 islands extending from Lombok, just east of Bali, to Timor. These islands, also known as the Lesser Sundas, are divided into two provinces. About 50 of the islands have been named. Lombok and Sumbawa are the major islands in the western region; Sumba, Flores and Timor are the major islands in the eastern province. Moving eastward through this chain of islands, the dry season lengthens and lush tropical landscape changes to more arid, rocky terrain.

Tourism in this area is increasing as lodgings and services improve. Tiny Komodo, located between Sumbawa and Flores draws visitors from around the world to observe its fearsome Komodo dragon, the giant carnivorous lizard. The staples of the more arid islands are corn, manioc, sorghum and millet as well as tubers such as taro. Water supplies are not sufficient to provide enough rice for daily consumption. *Ayam* Taliwang, grilled, butterflied chicken served with hot chili pepper sauce, is a specialty of Lombok. Salads made with water spinach (*kangkung*) are also local favorites. *Sepat ayam,* shredded chicken in a coconut-based sour sauce with unripe mango is a specialty of Sumbawa. On the small islands of Roti and Savu, the sweet sap of the *lontar* palm (*tuak manis*) provides the main sustenance of the people. That which isn't consumed as a beverage—fresh and mildly fermented or distilled into sopi, a strong alcohol—is processed into a type of rock candy or palm sugar (*gula batu*) or a type of molasses (*gula lemping*). East Timor, a former Portuguese colony, has items on the menu reflecting its European colonial heritage. Two such favorites are *caldeirada,* a hearty fish stew with vegetables, and *bolo delicio de caramelo,* a rich frosted cake.

The Malukus: The Spice Islands

About a thousand islands comprise Maluku (formerly the Moluccas), Indonesia's most famous islands—the Spice Islands. It is the only province in the archipelago that is more water than land. Ambon, Ternate, Tidore and the Bandas are the primary tourist destinations in this island cluster. The only city of size is Ambon, the provincial capital of Maluku on the island of the same name.

Sago, manioc (cassava), taro, yams, corn, sugar cane, almond-like *kanari* nuts and plantain are main staples of the islands. Copra, dried coconut meat, is produced for cooking oil. Cloves, nutmeg and mace are still important crops, but they are not as lucrative as in the past. Sago, a starchy, low-protein food, is derived from the soft pith of the sago (*sagu*) palm. Water is added to pulverized pith to release its starch, which is then dried and eaten as porridge (*papeda*). Bread is also made with sago flour. Droplets or "pearls" of sago, called *mutiara,* are made by sieving moistened sago that has been colored pink or green. When dried, the droplets are used in desserts and drinks. Manioc leaves mixed with coconut milk are also popular. Other regional treats are *bagea,* a brittle cake made of sago flour and *kohu kohu,* a salad of smoked tuna. *Colo colo* is an Ambonese sweet-sour sauce for fish, made with chili peppers and citrus fruits, and *dabu dabu* is an Ambonese raw vegetable salad of chopped tomatoes, chili peppers, shallots, *kanari* nuts and fermented fish paste. In North Sulawesi, interestingly, this is the name of a condiment served with whole roast pig or grilled fish. It contains chili peppers, tomatoes, *bakasang,* a paste of fermented sardine or tuna intestines, and the juice of *lemon cui,* a citrus fruit grown in that area.

Irian Jaya

Irian Jaya (formerly Dutch New Guinea) is Indonesia's largest and most primitive province. It consists of the western half of New Guinea, the world's second largest island. Most of the inhabitants are tribal people; the rest are transmigrants from overpopulated islands in the archipelago. Jayapura is the provincial capital. The few tourists that come to visit generally travel deep into the interior to visit indigenous groups, especially the aboriginal Dani tribe in the central highlands.

Sweet potatoes, sago, taro, bananas and tobacco are main crops. Trunks of some sago palms are allowed to rot so beetles infest the pith and lay eggs. The resulting grubs are a delicacy and protein source, as are chickens, pigs, and river crawfish. There is little in the way of regional Indonesian food since the transmigrants brought with them their own local specialties.

Traditional cooking utensils. Left: a coconut grater with rows of tiny metal nails; middle: a ladle made out of a piece of coconut shell; and right: a wooden spatula.

Tastes of Indonesia

You are encouraged to try some of these classic Indonesian recipes before you leave home. This is a wonderful and immediately rewarding way to preview the extraordinary cuisine of Indonesia. Most of the special Indonesian ingredients necessary for these recipes are available in the United States (see *Resources,* p. 59). Satisfactory substitutes are given for unavailable ones.

APPETIZERS/SNACKS

Sambal Goreng Tempe

Spicy, sweet-sour strips of fried bean cake. Serves 6.
The recipe for this crunchy snack or condiment was provided by Bill Dalton, founder of the *Moon Travel Guides* and author of the classic *Indonesian Handbook.* This preparation can be sprinkled over any side dish or rice. It is a favorite treat for Indonesian children, who eat it like candy.

> 3 4-OUNCE PACKAGES FERMENTED SOYBEAN CAKES (TEMPE),* CUT INTO
>   STRIPS ABOUT ¼-INCH SQUARE AND 1–2 INCHES LONG
>
> 1 CUP OIL FOR DEEP-FRYING
>
> 2 SHALLOTS, PEELED AND THINLY SLICED
>
> 4 CLOVES GARLIC, CHOPPED
>
> 1 TEASPOON FRESH LAOS,* PEELED AND SLICED
>
> ½ TEASPOON SHRIMP PASTE (*TRASI*)*
>
> 2 RED CHILI PEPPERS, THINLY SLICED
>
> 1 TABLESPOON OIL
>
> 5 TABLESPOONS PALM SUGAR* OR BROWN SUGAR
>
> 2–3 TABLESPOONS WATER
>
> 1 TABLESPOON TAMARIND CONCENTRATE*
>
> SALT TO TASTE
>
> 6 BIRD'S EYE CHILI PEPPERS FOR DECORATION

[Sambal Goreng Tempe, *continued*]

Deep-fry strips of tempe in hot oil, frying about ¼ of the strips at a time. Remove strips with slotted spoon, drain on paper towels and set aside. In a separate pan, sauté shallots, garlic, laos, shrimp paste and chili peppers in 1 tablespoon oil for 2–3 minutes, over medium-low heat. Add palm sugar, water and tamarind, and stir until the palm sugar has dissolved. Add strips of tempe and stir frequently until the sauce has reduced and caramelized. Season to taste with salt and decorate with bird's eye chili peppers.

*Available at markets carrying Asian food products; also see *Resources* (p. 59) for mail-order sources of Indonesian foods.

Surya's Tempe

Fried strips of bean cake. Serves 6.

This version of a snack made of soybean cake was provided by Madé Surya, co-owner with his wife, Judy Slattum, of Danu Enterprises, a travel agency specializing in travel to Indonesia. Surya is from Denpesar, Bali.

½ CUP SHALLOTS, THINLY SLICED

5 CLOVES GARLIC, MINCED

2 TEASPOONS VEGETABLE OIL

3 4-OUNCE PACKAGES FERMENTED SOYBEAN CAKES (TEMPE),* CUT INTO
 STRIPS ABOUT ¼-INCH SQUARE AND ABOUT 2 INCHES LONG

VEGETABLE OIL FOR DEEP-FRYING

¼ CUP SOY SAUCE

2 TABLESPOONS CHILI PEPPERS, CRUSHED

2 TABLESPOONS PALM SUGAR* OR BROWN SUGAR

DASH OF TABASCO SAUCE

Fry shallots and garlic in oil until golden and crispy. Remove with a slotted spoon and drain on paper towels to absorb oil. Set aside. Deep-fry tempe in hot oil, preferably in a wok, until golden.

While it is frying, mix together soy sauce, chili peppers, palm sugar and Tabasco. Remove tempe from wok and drain on paper towels.

Clean wok and then put tempe back in. Add sauce mixture and stir over low heat until all the sauce is absorbed. Then add fried shallots and garlic, and mix well.

*Available at markets carrying Asian food products; also see *Resources* (p. 59) for mail-order sources of Indonesian foods.

Gimbal Udang

Shrimp fritters. Makes 16.

This recipe was provided by John Hartanto, from Semarang, Central Java. With his wife Mien, he runs Tedjo Express USA, a travel agency in Los Angeles specializing in Indonesian destinations.

½ POUND RAW SHRIMP, DEVEINED AND CHOPPED INTO ½-INCH PIECES

4 SCALLIONS, FINELY CHOPPED

1 CUP BEAN SPROUTS, WASHED AND PATTED DRY; REMOVE ROOT TIPS

5 TABLESPOONS WHITE FLOUR

¾ CUP THICK COCONUT MILK*

1 TEASPOON CORIANDER, GROUND

1 TEASPOON SALT

Combine flour and coconut milk, and blend until smooth. Add the rest of the ingredients, mixing well. Prepare skillet with enough oil for deep-frying. Put one heaping tablespoon of the mixture into hot oil and fry until golden. Repeat with the remaining mixture, frying one fritter at a time.

*Bottled or canned coconut milk can be substituted.

Soups

Sop Buntut

Oxtail soup. Serves 4.

This recipe was provided by Ibu Gina Rosalina from Bandung, West Java, a home economist, catering and banquet menu planner and administrative assistant of William F & B Management, Jakarta, Java.

2 POUNDS OXTAIL, CUT INTO 1-INCH PIECES

6½ CUPS WATER

1 TEASPOON NUTMEG

5 CLOVES

SALT TO TASTE

1 TEASPOON PEPPER

4 MEDIUM POTATOES, CUBED

4–5 MEDIUM CARROTS, SLICED

5 CLOVES GARLIC, CHOPPED

1 MEDIUM ONION, CHOPPED

[Sop Buntut, *continued*]

2–3 TEASPOONS BUTTER

¼ CUP LEEK (WHITE PART ONLY), FINELY CHOPPED

⅛ CUP CELERY, FINELY CHOPPED

1 TOMATO, SLICED

Put oxtail in boiling water, reduce the heat to medium and cook until meat is tender, about 3 hours. Skim off fat. Add nutmeg, cloves, salt, pepper, potatoes and carrots. Sauté garlic and onion until golden and add to soup. Cook about 10 minutes more, or until carrots and potatoes are done. Serve garnished with leeks, celery and sliced tomato.

Soto Bandung

Clear beef soup with lemon grass and daikon radish. Serves 4.

The recipe for this soup was contributed by Dwito Nugroho Satmoko, award-winning chef at the Chedi Hotel in Bandung, West Java. Plan ahead: the soybeans need to soak in water overnight.

½ CUP DRIED SOYBEANS, SOAKED IN WATER OVERNIGHT

1 POUND BEEF BRISKET (CAN SUBSTITUTE BEEF SHANK),

CUT IN ½-INCH CUBES

FRESH GINGER, ABOUT 2½ INCHES LONG, CRUSHED

1 STALK LEMON GRASS,* WASHED AND CUT INTO 3 PIECES,

EACH ABOUT 3 INCHES LONG, CRUSHED

1 LARGE DAIKON RADISH, WASHED AND PEELED

4½ CUPS WHITE BEEF STOCK† OR WATER

3–4 SHALLOTS, PEELED AND MINCED

2 CLOVES GARLIC, MINCED

SALT AND WHITE PEPPER TO TASTE

5 TEASPOONS VEGETABLE OIL

3 TABLESPOONS INDONESIAN SWEET SOY SAUCE*

3 TEASPOONS WHITE VINEGAR OR LIME JUICE

⅛ CUP CELERY LEAVES, FINELY SLICED

1 LEEK, FINELY SLICED

10 BIRD'S EYE CHILI PEPPERS

1 LEMON, QUARTERED

Put meat, ginger, lemon grass and whole radish into beef stock or water, and bring to a boil. Sauté shallots and garlic, seasoned with salt and pepper, in 2 teaspoons oil until golden. Add to boiling mixture.

Drain soybeans and fry in 1 tablespoon oil until golden, about 3–4 minutes. Set aside on paper towels to absorb excess oil.

Reduce heat to low, and simmer soup. Add soy sauce and vinegar or lime juice, and continue to cook until the meat is tender. Correct the seasonings. Remove the radish and cut crosswise into slices about ¼ inch thick. Remove and discard the ginger and lemon grass.

To make the condiment, or *sambal*, boil the chili peppers in a small amount of soup stock for about 1 minute. Remove and mince. Add salt to taste.

To serve soup, put some fried soybeans and slices of radish into individual bowls and cover with soup. Garnish with a sprinkle of celery leaves and leek.

If desired, squeeze some lemon juice into the soup and add a small dollop of the minced chili peppers.

*Available at markets carrying Asian food products; also see *Resources* (p. 59) for mail-order sources of Indonesian foods.

†Bones for stock are blanched, not roasted until brown, before making the stock.

VEGETABLES

Sayur Lodeh

Vegetables in a thin sauce with coconut milk. This Jakarta-style variation contains eggplant and cabbage. Serves 4.

This recipe was provided by Irma Nawangwulan, who is studying for her MBA at Edgewood College in Madison, Wisconsin. She is from Jakarta, Java.

2 TEASPOONS VEGETABLE OIL

2 EGGPLANTS, CUT INTO SMALL CUBES

2 MEDIUM YELLOW ONIONS, SLICED

2 SHALLOTS, SLICED

1 CLOVE GARLIC, MINCED

1 CUP CABBAGE, SHREDDED

1 *SALAM* LEAF* OR BAY LEAF

1 TEASPOON SHRIMP PASTE (*TRASI*)*

1 TEASPOON TAMARIND CONCENTRATE*†

½ TEASPOON CUMIN, GROUND

[Sayur Lodeh, *continued*]

½ TEASPOON CORIANDER, GROUND

1 CUP CHICKEN OR BEEF BROTH

1 12-OUNCE CAN COCONUT MILK

1–2 TABLESPOONS SUGAR

SALT AND PEPPER TO TASTE

DRIED, FRIED SHALLOT FLAKES*

Heat oil in wok or frying pan. Sauté onions, shallots and garlic for a few minutes. Add cabbage and stir fry for about 2 minutes. Then add other ingredients except coconut milk and eggplant. Sauté for about 5 minutes. Add eggplant and mix well. Stir fry for 2–3 minutes. Add coconut and cook for about 8 minutes. The eggplant should be soft, but not mushy. Garnish with shallot flakes. Serve with steamed rice and a chili pepper condiment.

*Available at markets carrying Asian food products; also see *Resources* (p. 59) for mail-order sources of Indonesian foods.

†Thick tamarind water can be substituted. To make, simmer ¼ pound tamarind pulp in about 1¼ cups water until half the liquid has evaporated. Remove seeds and pieces of pods, if any, by sieving. The unused portion can be stored in the refrigerator for about 2 weeks or frozen.

VEGETABLE SALADS

Urap

Mixed vegetable salad dressed with a coconut/spice mixture, traditionally served for lunch with steamed, sticky (glutinous) rice. Serves 6.

The recipe for this typical Betawi (ethnic group indigenous to Jakarta) dish was provided by Ibu Aisyah Sidik Surkatty, a homemaker and mother of 11 from Tegal, Central Java. Now living in Jakarta, she is happiest in the kitchen with family members, preparing feasts for Muslim religious festivals as well as everyday meals.

3 BUNCHES SPINACH (ABOUT 6–7 CUPS)

¼ HEAD CABBAGE, COARSELY SHREDDED (ABOUT 3 CUPS)

5–6 CUPS BEAN SPROUTS

20 YARD-LONG BEANS,* CUT INTO 1-INCH PIECES (ABOUT 2½ CUPS)

1 RIPE COCONUT WITH COCONUT WATER, ABOUT 5-INCH DIAMETER†

5 SHALLOTS

4 FRESH RED CHILI PEPPERS, 4 INCHES LONG

1½-INCH PIECE FRESH AROMATIC GINGER (LESSER GALANGAL)††

1–2 TEASPOONS SUGAR, TO TASTE

1–2 TEASPOONS SALT, TO TASTE

Remove the stems from the spinach leaves and discard. Parboil spinach leaves, cabbage, bean sprouts and beans separately and cool to room temperature. Mix together. Shred the coconut meat in a food processor.† Set aside about 1½–2 cups, and freeze the remainder for future use. Mound coconut in a steamer and place next to it whole shallots, chili peppers and aromatic ginger. Steaming releases the flavor and slightly cooks the spices. Steam until spice items are softened, but not thoroughly cooked. Remove shallots, chili peppers and aromatic ginger. Grind with a mortar and pestle until thoroughly smashed and mixed. Add coconut to spice mixture and stir until well mixed. The chili peppers redden the coconut. Mix parboiled vegetables with coconut and spice mixture. Add sugar and salt to taste and serve at room temperature.

*Available at markets carrying Asian food products; also see *Resources* (p. 59) for mail-order sources of Indonesian foods. Can substitute ordinary green beans.

†See instructions on how to crack open a coconut and shred the meat in the miscellaneous category at the end of this chapter, under "Coconut Milk."

††Available at markets carrying Asian food products; also see *Resources* (p. 59) for mail-order sources of Indonesian foods. Don't substitute fresh ginger.

Jukut Urap

Mixed vegetable salad, Balinese style. Serves 6–8.

Ken Fish, owner of Absolute Asia, a travel agency in New York City specializing in custom-designed travel arrangements to Asia, provided this recipe. It is an example of Balinese vegetarian cooking.

3½ OUNCES HEAD CABBAGE, CUT INTO 1-INCH SQUARES

3½ OUNCES SPINACH

3½ OUNCES YARD-LONG BEANS,* CUT INTO 1-INCH PIECES*

3½ OUNCES BEAN SPROUTS

2 TABLESPOONS SHALLOTS, CHOPPED

2 TABLESPOONS VEGETABLE OIL

3 CLOVES GARLIC, MINCED

1 SMALL TOMATO, PEELED AND CHOPPED

3 HOT RED CHILI PEPPERS, SLICED

3 KAFFIR LIME LEAVES,† VERY FINELY CHOPPED

½ TEASPOON CANE SUGAR

1 TABLESPOON COCONUT, GRATED

[Jukut Urap, *continued*]

¼ TEASPOON SALT

¼ TEASPOON BLACK PEPPER, CRUSHED

JUICE OF 1 LIME

Wash and parboil cabbage, spinach, beans and bean sprouts separately. Cabbage and beans should be tender. Drain and cool. Gently stir-fry shallots in oil until crisp and golden. Remove and set aside. Stir-fry garlic until aroma arises. Add tomato and chili peppers, and stir-fry until tender.

Mix parboiled and stir-fried ingredients together in a salad bowl. Add lime leaves, sugar and coconut, and mix thoroughly. Season to taste with salt, pepper and lime juice. Serve at room temperature.

*Available at markets carrying Asian food products; also see *Resources* (p. 59) for mail-order sources of Indonesian foods. Can substitute ordinary green beans.

†Available at markets carrying Asian food products; also see *Resources* (p. 59) for mail-order sources of Indonesian foods.

Gado Gado

Steamed vegetables with peanut sauce. Serves 4.

This recipe was contributed by Ibu Wayan, owner of Cafe Wayan in Ubud, Bali.

2–3 CUPS FRESH SPINACH, LOOSELY PACKED

¼ POUND FRESH GREEN BEANS, CUT INTO 1-INCH LENGTHS

½ POUND TOFU, CUT INTO ¾-INCH CUBES

1 CUP BEAN SPROUTS

Peanut sauce

CORN OIL FOR DEEP-FRYING

1 CUP PEANUTS, RAW

1 CLOVE GARLIC, CHOPPED

2 LARGE SHALLOTS, CHOPPED

1 LARGE RED CHILI PEPPER, CHOPPED

1 MEDIUM TOMATO, CHOPPED

1 TEASPOON SALT

1 TEASPOON SOY SAUCE

1 CUP WATER

JUICE OF ONE LIME

Garnish

1 CUCUMBER, PEELED AND SLICED CROSSWISE

2 HARD-BOILED EGGS, SLICED CROSSWISE

Steam beans for 5 minutes. Add tofu and steam about 5 minutes. Then add spinach and bean sprouts and steam 10 minutes more, or until the beans are crisp-tender. Arrange vegetables on a platter.

To make the sauce, deep-fry peanuts 3–4 minutes in corn oil. Drain and cool. Using a food processor, grind peanuts to a powder and set aside. Sauté garlic, red onion and chili pepper for 1–2 minutes in 1 tablespoon of the oil used to fry peanuts. Add tomato, salt, soy sauce and water, and bring to a boil. Add pulverized peanuts and simmer until sauce thickens, about 10 minutes. Add lime juice and blend well. Put sauce on top of the vegetables, in the center of the platter. Garnish with egg and cucumber slices. Serve with steamed rice.

Main Dishes

Rendang Ayam
Chicken "long-cooked" in spicy coconut. Serves 4–6.
The recipe for this dish was provided by Sri Owen, from her cookbook entitled *Indonesian Regional Cooking.* Her grandmother used this recipe when Ms. Owen was a small child in Padang Panjang, West Sumatra.

7½ CUPS COCONUT MILK*

6 SHALLOTS OR 1 LARGE ONION, FINELY CHOPPED

4 CLOVES GARLIC, CHOPPED

2 TEASPOONS FRESH GINGER, FINELY CHOPPED

1–3 TEASPOONS *SAMBAL ULEK*†, OR 1 TEASPOON CHILI POWDER

1 TEASPOON TURMERIC, GROUND

1 STALK OF LEMON GRASS,† CUT INTO 3 PIECES AND BRUISED

1-INCH PIECE OF GALANGAL (LAOS),† OR ½ TEASPOON POWDER

2 *SALAM* LEAVES† OR BAY LEAVES

1 TURMERIC LEAF (OPTIONAL)†

1–2 TEASPOONS SALT

1 CHICKEN, WEIGHING ABOUT 4 POUNDS, CUT INTO 8 PIECES

2 TABLESPOONS VERY THICK TAMARIND WATER (OPTIONAL)††

Put all ingredients except the chicken and tamarind water into a large saucepan or wok. Bring to a boil. Reduce the heat and simmer gently for an hour, stirring

[Rendang Ayam, *continued*]

occasionally to reduce the liquid. Add the chicken pieces and tamarind water, if used, and continue cooking as before, stirring occasionally, for another 1–1½ hours. The liquid will be quite thick. Lower the heat a little and continue to simmer, stirring often, until the sauce is very thick and appears to be oily. This is because the coconut milk, after long cooking, has become oil, with the *blondo,* the oil's sediment, well blended with the spices.

Increase the heat and continue cooking, stirrring often, until all the oil has been absorbed by the meat and sediment. Remove and discard the chunk of galangal and pieces of lemon grass. Adjust the seasonings. Serve hot with plenty of rice, accompanied by any green vegetable.

*Bottled or canned coconut milk can be substituted.

†Available at markets carrying Asian food products; also see *Resources* (p. 59) for mail-order sources of Indonesian foods.

††Available at markets carrying Asian food products; also see *Resources* (p. 59) for mail-order sources of Indonesian foods. To make, simmer ¼ pound tamarind pulp in about 1¼ cups water until half the liquid has evaporated. Remove seeds and pieces of pods, if any, by sieving. The unused portion can be frozen or stored in the refrigerator for about 2 weeks.

Sate Manis

Sweet and spicy strips of marinated meat grilled on skewers. Serves 4–6.

The recipe for this classic Indonesian dish was provided by Marilyn Staff, co-founder of Bolder Adventures, an agency in Colorado specializing in Southeast Asia travel. You will need 25 bamboo skewers, soaked in cold water about two hours beforehand to prevent burning on the grill. Plan ahead because the meat marinates for 2 hours to overnight before being cooked.

> 1½ POUNDS BEEFSTEAK (FILLET OR RUMP STEAK)
>
> 1 TABLESPOON PALM SUGAR* OR BROWN SUGAR
>
> 1 CLOVE GARLIC, CRUSHED
>
> ½ TEASPOON SALT
>
> 2 TABLESPOONS INDONESIAN SWEET SOY SAUCE (*KECAP MANIS*)*
>
> 1 TABLESPOON PEANUT OIL
>
> 1 TABLESPOON CUMIN, GROUND
>
> *Sate Sauce*
>
> ½ CUP PEANUT SAUCE (SEE RECIPE BELOW)
>
> 2 TABLESPOONS TAMARIND WATER* OR LEMON JUICE

3 FRESH, SMALL, GREEN, HOT CHILI PEPPERS, GROUND

¾ TABLESPOON WATER

Peanut Sauce

7 TABLESPOONS PEANUT OIL

6 CLOVES GARLIC, MINCED, OR 1 TEASPOON DRIED GARLIC POWDER

1 MEDIUM ONION, CHOPPED, OR 2 TABLESPOONS DRIED ONION FLAKES

2 LARGE, DRIED CHILI PEPPERS

1 TEASPOON DRIED SHRIMP PASTE (*TRASI*)*

1 TABLESPOON LEMON JUICE, FRESHLY SQUEEZED

1 TABLESPOON INDONESIAN SWEET SOY SAUCE (*KECAP MANIS*)*

12 OUNCES CRUNCHY PEANUT BUTTER

1½ TABLESPOON PALM SUGAR* OR BROWN SUGAR

⅓ CUP COCONUT MILK (OPTIONAL)

Cut beef into thin strips, about 1 inch wide and ¼ inch thick. Thread loosely onto bamboo skewers. Combine sugar, garlic, salt, soy sauce, oil and cumin. Stir until sugar and salt dissolve. Pour over meat in shallow glass dish, cover and allow meat to marinate in the refrigerator for at least two hours or overnight. Cook over hot glowing charcoal or under oven broiler for 15 minutes. During cooking, turn skewers every 5 minutes and brush with marinade. Serve hot, covered with *sate* sauce.

To make the peanut sauce, an ingredient of *sate* sauce, heat oil in small wok or frying pan. Fry garlic, onions and chili peppers for a few minutes. Remove with strainer and set aside. Remove oil from heat and cool. This is very important or you will have an explosion when you add the liquid. Add peanut butter, lemon juice, shrimp paste and soy sauce to the oil. Stir until well blended. Crush fried garlic, onions and chili peppers, and add to mixture. Use as is, or thin with coconut milk for a more liquid texture. To make the *sate* sauce, combine all ingredients and pour over hot meat as soon as it is taken off the grill.

*Available at markets carrying Asian food products; also see *Resources* (p. 59) for mail-order sources of Indonesian foods.

Lawar

The hash-like Balinese festival dish made with finely chopped ingredients. Serves 10. The recipe for this vegetable and fruit version of *lawar* was provided by Ibu Okawati, owner of Okawati's restaurant and bungalows in Ubud, Bali.

½ POUND YARD-LONG BEANS,* WASHED AND TRIMMED

1½ POUNDS GREEN (UNRIPE) PAPAYA, PEELED AND CUT INTO 1-INCH CUBES

[Lawar, *continued*]

1 12-OUNCE CAN GREEN JACKFRUIT,† RINSED AND DRAINED

2 LARGE SHALLOTS, FINELY CHOPPED

4 LARGE RED MILD CHILI PEPPERS, FINELY CHOPPED

1 MEDIUM GREEN HOT CHILI PEPPER, FINELY CHOPPED

4 TEASPOONS OIL

4 CANDLENUTS (KEMIRI)†

½ TEASPOON CARAWAY SEEDS

1 TEASPOON CORIANDER, GROUND

¼ TEASPOON WHITE PEPPER

½ TEASPOON BLACK PEPPER

1 TEASPOON DRIED CHILI PEPPERS

¼ TEASPOON CLOVES

¼ TEASPOON NUTMEG

¼ TEASPOON AROMATIC GINGER (KENCUR)†

1 TEASPOON SALT

4 CLOVES GARLIC, MINCED

1 TEASPOON SHRIMP PASTE†

JUICE OF ½ LIME

1 KAFFIR LIME LEAF,† FINELY CHOPPED

MEAT FROM ½ COCONUT, REMOVED FROM SHELL, UNPEELED

Boil beans 5 minutes or until tender but not soft. Drain and set aside. Steam papaya 20 minutes, until tender but not soft. Drain.

Finely chop beans, papaya and jackfruit, mix together in a large bowl and set aside. Sauté onions and chili peppers in 2 teaspoons oil until limp, and set aside.

Sauté candlenuts in 1 teaspoon oil until golden brown, drain and set aside. Grind caraway seeds to a powder with a mortar and pestle. Add coriander, white and black pepper, dried chili pepper, cloves, nutmeg, aromatic ginger and salt, and blend well. Remove and set aside.

Grind candlenuts to a paste with the mortar and pestle. Add garlic and shrimp paste and mix well. Add blended dry spices and mix well. Sauté the mixture of dry and wet spices in 1 teaspoon oil for a few minutes and set aside.

Toast the pieces of coconut meat, brown skin side down, for about 5 minutes on a grill to produce a nutty flavor. Cool. Remove brown skin and discard. Grate coconut and set aside.

Add the sautéed onions and chili peppers to chopped fruits and vegetables and blend well. Add sautéed spice mixture, coconut, lime leaf and lime juice, and toss together. Serve at room temperature.

*Available at markets carrying Asian food products. Can substitute ordinary green beans.

†Available at markets carrying Asian food products; also see *Resources* (p. 59) for mail-order sources of Indonesian foods.

Pindang Serani Salm

Salmon simmered in spicy broth. Serves 10.
This recipe was provided by William W. Wongso, owner of William F & B Management, Jakarta, Java.

> 4 POUNDS FRESH SALMON, WHOLE OR ½ SALMON
>
> 8 TABLESPOONS SHALLOTS, CHOPPED
>
> 4 TABLESPOONS GARLIC, CHOPPED
>
> 1 STALK LEMON GRASS,* CUT INTO 3-INCH PIECES, BRUISED
>
> 5 TABLESPOONS FRESH TURMERIC,* CHOPPED
>
> 5 TABLESPOONS FRESH GREATER GALANGAL (LAOS),* CHOPPED
>
> 10 TABLESPOONS FRESH GINGER,* CHOPPED
>
> 10 KAFFIR LIME LEAVES*
>
> 5 *SALAM* LEAVES*†
>
> JUICE OF 1 LARGE LEMON
>
> 20 BIRD'S EYE CHILI PEPPERS*
>
> 7 *BELIMBING WULUH,*†† CUT IN HALF LENGTHWISE
>
> 8 CUPS WATER

In a pan large enough to hold the salmon, sauté shallots and garlic until golden brown. Add water and remaining ingredients except the fish, chili peppers and tart fruit called *belimbing wuluh.*

Boil, then add salmon. Reduce heat and simmer, uncovered, until salmon is cooked. Remove from pan and garnish with chili peppers and *belimbing wuluh.*

*Available at markets carrying Asian food products; also see *Resources* (p. 59) for mail-order sources of Indonesian foods.

†Can substitute bay leaves.

††Can substitute lemon slices.

Ikan Woku

Baked and grilled fish in a mixture of spices typical of Sulawesi. Serves 4.

Beverly and Syamsul Bachri, from the city of Ujung Pandang, South Sulawesi, provided the recipe for this dish. They own and operate Bachri's Restaurant in Pittsburgh, Pennsylvania, specializing in Indonesian dishes, and have a mail-order business offering ingredients and sauces from Southeast Asia, particularly Indonesia.

1 OR 2 WHOLE FISH, 2 POUNDS TOTAL, CLEANED

    (MULLET, SNAPPER OR MACKEREL WORK BEST)

3 BIRD'S EYE CHILI PEPPERS (VERY HOT)

3 CANDLENUTS*

1 1-INCH PIECE GINGER ROOT

1 LARGE RIPE TOMATO, PEELED AND CHOPPED

½ TEASPOON TURMERIC, GROUND

JUICE OF 1 LIME

2 TABLESPOONS FRESH MINT, CHOPPED

4 TABLESPOONS SCALLIONS, CHOPPED

2 TEASPOONS SALT

Using a food processor, grind the chili peppers, candlenuts and ginger together into a paste. Add to the rest of the ingredients except the fish and blend well. Rub the mixture onto the fish, inside and out. Wrap the fish in foil and refrigerate for at least 30 minutes. (In Sulawesi, the fish would be wrapped in a banana leaf.) Bake at 375°F for 15 minutes.

Just before serving, unwrap the fish and broil for 5 minutes, or until done.

*Available at markets carrying Asian food products; also see *Resources* (p. 59) for mail-order sources of Indonesian foods.

Nasi Goreng

Indonesian fried rice. Serves 4–6.

This recipe was contributed by Ibu Wayan, owner of Cafe Wayan in Ubud, Bali.

4 TABLESPOONS CORN OIL

1 TABLESPOON GARLIC, MINCED

1 LARGE RED CHILI PEPPER, CHOPPED

¼ POUND SHRIMP, DEVEINED AND CUT INTO SMALL PIECES

1 CUP HEAD CABBAGE, SHREDDED

⅛ POUND FRESH GREEN BEANS, CUT CROSSWISE IN SMALL PIECES

2½ CUPS STEAMED RICE, COLD

1 TOMATO, CHOPPED

2 TABLESPOONS TOMATO SAUCE

2 TABLESPOONS INDONESIAN SWEET SOY SAUCE (*KECAP MANIS*)*

1 TABLESPOON REGULAR SOY SAUCE

4–6 EGGS, FRIED

In a wok or frying pan, sauté garlic in oil over medium heat for 1–2 minutes. Add chili pepper and sauté about 1 minute. Add shrimp and sauté about 2 minutes. Then add cabbage and green beans, and sauté 5 more minutes, or until beans are tender.

Reduce heat to low, and mix in the rice, tomato, tomato sauce and both types of soy sauce. Blend well and fry until hot. Serve each portion with a fried egg on top.

*Available at markets carrying Asian food products; also see *Resources* (p. 59) for mail-order sources of Indonesian foods.

Ayam Panggang

Indonesian roast chicken. Serves 4.

The recipe for this dish was contributed by Ibu Tuti Soenardi from Surabaya, East Java. She is a nutritionist, cookbook author, host of television cooking shows and director of the Culinary and Nutrition Foundation (Yayasan Gizi Kuliner Indonesia) in Jakarta, Java.

2–3 POUND CHICKEN, CUT IN HALF LENGTHWISE

2 CUPS THICK COCONUT MILK*

10 SHALLOTS

5 CLOVES GARLIC

6 RED CHILI PEPPERS

10 CANDLENUTS†

1 TEASPOON SHRIMP PASTE (*TRASI*)†

1½ TEASPOONS SALT

2 TEASPOONS PALM SUGAR† OR BROWN SUGAR

2 THIN SLICES FRESH LAOS†

2 STALKS LEMON GRASS,† BRUISED

1 TABLESPOON TAMARIND CONCENTRATE††

[Ayam Panggang, *continued*]

Grill the chicken gently, skin side up, over or under low heat until almost golden. Mix together shallots, garlic, chili peppers, candlenuts, shrimp paste, salt and palm sugar in a food processor and grind to a paste. Add paste, laos and lemon grass to coconut milk and bring to a boil. Simmer until mixture is almost dry, about 30 minutes, stirring frequently. Remove and discard laos and lemon grass.

Rub the spice mixture on the chicken halves. Grill the chicken again, basting with remaining spice mixture. When meat is done, serve hot or cold with steamed rice.

*Bottled or canned coconut milk can be substituted.

†Available at markets carrying Asian food products; also see *Resources* (p. 59) for mail-order sources of Indonesian foods.

††Available at markets carrying Asian food products; also see *Resources* (p. 59) for mail-order sources of Indonesian foods. To make, simmer ¼ pound tamarind pulp in about 1¼ cups water until half the liquid has evaporated. Remove seeds and pieces of pods, if any, by sieving. The unused portion can be stored in the refrigerator for about 2 weeks or frozen.

Ayam Woku

Chicken cooked in a spice mixture typical of Sulawesi. Serves 4.

This recipe was provided by Ibu Bernadeth Ratulangi, owner of Gardenia Homestay in Tomohon, North Sulawesi.

2 POUNDS CHICKEN, CUT INTO 12 PIECES

1½ CUPS LEEK, CHOPPED

6 TABLESPOONS FRESH GINGER, PEELED AND CHOPPED

1 STALK LEMON GRASS,* CUT INTO 3 PIECES, BRUISED

1 OUNCE FRESH LAOS,* PEELED AND SLICED

5 KAFFIR LIME LEAVES*

10 GREEN CHILI PEPPERS, FINELY MINCED

10 BIRD'S EYE CHILI PEPPERS (VERY HOT), FINELY MINCED

1 TABLESPOON GARLIC, MINCED

1 TABLESPOON SHALLOTS, FINELY CHOPPED

SALT TO TASTE

5 TABLESPOONS COOKING OIL

½ CUP WATER

1 OUNCE FRESH BASIL LEAVES (CHOOSE SMALL ONES FOR STRONGER FLAVOR)

Sauté all herbs and spices except basil in oil in a heavy saucepan. Add chicken and water, and cover pan. Cook over medium heat, stirring occasionally, for 30 minutes or until done. Add fresh basil after meat is cooked. Remove and discard lemon grass, Kaffir lime leaves and laos before serving.

*Available at markets carrying Asian food products; also see *Resources* (p. 59) for mail-order sources of Indonesian foods.

Paruik

Egg sausages in spicy coconut milk sauce. Serves 4–6.

This recipe was provided by Ibu Hayatinufus Afit L. Tobing from East Java. She is a home economist, cookbook author and Indonesian culinary consultant in Jakarta, Java.

> 3 12-INCH LENGTHS OF PORK CASINGS, CLEANED*
>
> 10 LARGE EGGS*
>
> ½ TEASPOON SALT
>
> ½ TEASPOON WHITE PEPPER, GROUND
>
> 5 OUNCES LONG RED CHILI PEPPERS, CHOPPED
>
> 2 TABLESPOONS FRESH LAOS,† CHOPPED
>
> 2 TEASPOONS FRESH GINGER, CHOPPED
>
> 2 TEASPOONS FRESH TURMERIC,† CHOPPED
>
> 2 TEASPOONS CORIANDER, GROUND
>
> ¼ TEASPOON CUMIN, GROUND
>
> 10 SHALLOTS, CHOPPED
>
> 1 TEASPOON SALT
>
> 4 CUPS THIN COCONUT MILK††
>
> 1 TURMERIC LEAF†
>
> 5 KAFFIR LIME LEAVES†
>
> 1 STALK LEMON GRASS† CUT INTO 3 PIECES, BRUISED
>
> 1–2 SLICES *ASAM GLUGUR* OR *ASAM KANDIS*‡
>
> 1 CUP THICK COCONUT MILK††

Tie one end of each piece of casing closed with string. Beat eggs with salt and pepper. Fill casings with egg mixture until ¾ full, and securely tie the open end with string. Cover filled casings with water in a large saucepan and gently simmer until the eggs harden. Remove and set aside in a warm place.

[Paruik, *continued*]

Grind chili peppers, laos, ginger, turmeric, coriander, cumin, shallots and salt in a food processor to form a paste. In a large saucepan, blend paste together with thin coconut milk, turmeric leaf, lime leaves, lemon grass and *asam glugur* or *asam kandis*. Boil gently, uncovered, stirring frequently, for about one hour or until the sauce thickens and becomes reduced. Add thick coconut milk and blend well. Reduce heat to simmer.

When sauce has cooled somewhat, add sausages. Continue to stir occasionally, being careful not to break casings. Remove sausages after about a half hour and keep warm. Continue simmering sauce until thick and somewhat oily. Serve sausages covered with sauce.

*The original recipe calls for beef casings and duck eggs.

†Available at markets carrying Asian food products; also see *Resources* (p. 59) for mail-order sources of Indonesian foods.

††Can substitute bottled or canned coconut milk.

‡Can substitute 2 tablespoons tamarind concentrate.

Opor Ayam

Chicken in white, coconut milk-based sauce. Serves 6.

This recipe was provided by Winifred Nyhus, who lived in Indonesia with her husband, Edward, for a total of 25 years in the following cities: Pematang Siantar, North Sumatra, Salatiga, Central Java and Yogyakarta, Java. Edward Nyhus was a professor in departments of theology at Christian universities in these towns.

> 1 3-POUND CHICKEN, CUT INTO 8–10 PIECES, WITH FAT REMOVED
>
> 2 TEASPOONS LEMON JUICE
>
> 2 TEASPOONS SALT
>
> 2 TABLESPOONS VEGETABLE OIL
>
> 2¼ CUPS COCONUT MILK*
>
> 2 CLOVES GARLIC, SLICED
>
> 3 SHALLOTS, SLICED
>
> 1½-INCH SLICE FRESH GINGER ROOT, CHOPPED
>
> 2 TEASPOONS CORIANDER
>
> ½ TEASPOON LAOS, GROUND
>
> ⅛ TEASPOON WHITE PEPPER, GROUND
>
> 1 3-INCH PIECE LEMON GRASS,† INCLUDING BULB, BRUISED

1 BAY LEAF

½ TEASPOON TURMERIC, GROUND

1 TEASPOON PALM SUGAR†

1 TABLESPOON TAMARIND CONCENTRATE††

Put chicken into a glass or stainless steel bowl, sprinkle with lemon juice and salt, turning pieces several times until the juice is well distributed. Cover and refrigerate until ready to use.

Pour ¼ cup coconut milk into a blender and set aside. Sauté the garlic, shallots and ginger root in 1 tablespoon oil, stirring constantly to prevent burning. When the shallots are soft, remove the mixture from the heat and add to the coconut milk in the blender. Blend until nearly smooth, then return mixture to the saucepan and add 1 tablespoon oil, coriander, laos, pepper, turmeric, lemon grass and bay leaf. Simmer for a few minutes, stirring constantly, until flavors are blended and liquid is reduced. Add chicken and stir, while frying over moderate heat, until the pieces are coated with the spice mixture. Add 1 cup coconut milk, tamarind and palm sugar. Cover, and simmer about 40 minutes or until chicken is cooked, but still firm. Add remaining coconut milk.

Uncover and cook over low heat, occasionally basting or turning pieces, until chicken is tender and sauce is slightly thickened.

*Can substitute bottled or canned coconut milk.

†Available at markets carrying Asian food products; also see *Resources* (p. 59) for mail-order sources of Indonesian foods.

††Available at markets carrying Asian food products; also see *Resources* (p. 59) for mail-order sources of Indonesian foods. To make, simmer ¼ pound tamarind pulp in about 1¼ cups water until half the liquid has evaporated. Remove seeds and pieces of pods, if any, by sieving. The unused portion can be stored in the refrigerator for about 2 weeks or frozen.

Tum Hati Ayam

Spicy chicken livers steamed in banana leaves. Makes about 20.

This recipe was provided by Bapak Gusti Nyoman Darte, owner of Warung CuCu in Campuan-Ubud, Bali.

1 POUND FRESH CHICKEN LIVERS, MINCED

2 TEASPOONS SHALLOTS, CHOPPED

1 LONG RED CHILI PEPPER, MINCED

1 CLOVE GARLIC, MINCED

⅛ TEASPOON AROMATIC GINGER (*KENCUR*)*

[Tum Hati Ayam, *continued*]

    ½ TEASPOON FRESH TURMERIC,* FINELY CHOPPED

    ½ TEASPOON FRESH GINGER,* FINELY CHOPPED

    ½ TEASPOON FRESH LAOS,* FINELY CHOPPED

    ¼ TEASPOON CORIANDER SEEDS, GROUND

    1 KAFFIR LIME LEAF,* FINELY CHOPPED

    1 *SALAM* LEAF,* FINELY CHOPPED

    ¼ TEASPOON SALT OR TO TASTE

    PINCH CLOVES

    PINCH CINNAMON

    PINCH NUTMEG

    PINCH WHITE PEPPER

    PINCH BLACK PEPPER

    ½ CUP FRESH COCONUT, GRATED

    BANANA LEAVES,* CUT INTO 3 INCH BY 8 INCH RECTANGLES

Blend all ingredients well. Place about 3 tablespoons of mixture in center of a banana leaf rectangle. Bring the four edges together and skewer "bundle" with a toothpick. Steam for 15 minutes or until done.

*Available at markets carrying Asian food products; also see *Resources* (p. 59) for mail-order sources of Indonesian foods.

DESSERTS

Kolak Pisang

Sweet banana compote. Serves 12.

This recipe was provided by Ibu Gina Rosalina from Bandung, West Java, a home economist, catering and banquet menu planner and administrative assistant of William F & B Management, Jakarta, Java.

    10 FIRM BANANAS, CUT IN HALF LENGTHWISE, THEN IN THIRDS

    2⅓ CUPS LOOSELY PACKED PALM SUGAR* OR BROWN SUGAR

    2¼ CUPS WATER

    1⅛ CUPS THICK COCONUT MILK†

    ½ TEASPOON SALT

    1 TABLESPOON CORNSTARCH DISSOLVED IN 2 TABLESPOONS WATER

    1 PIECE *DAUN PANDAN,* ABOUT 4 INCHES LONG

Boil water, palm sugar and *pandan* leaf until syrupy, stirring frequently. Reduce heat, and slowly add coconut milk, salt and dissolved cornstarch. Add bananas and simmer until sauce thickens. Remove and discard *pandan* leaf before serving.

*Available at markets carrying Asian food products; also see *Resources* (p. 59) for mail-order sources of Indonesian foods.

†Bottled or canned coconut milk can be substituted.

Kelepon

Small balls filled with palm sugar. Makes 12–14.

These popular tidbits are eaten as a dessert or snack. The brown sugar filling liquifies during cooking. If you try to bite into one instead of popping it into your mouth whole, the juicy brown sugar probably will squirt out.

> 1⅛ CUPS STICKY (GLUTINOUS) RICE FLOUR*
>
> ½ CUP WATER
>
> GREEN FOOD COLORING
>
> 5–6 TEASPOONS VEGETABLE OIL
>
> ¼ CUP PALM SUGAR,* OR BROWN SUGAR
>
> 6 CUPS BOILING WATER
>
> 1 CUP COCONUT, FINELY GRATED

Put a small drop of food coloring into the water used for the dough, and mix well. Dough should be a very light green. Blend rice flour, colored water and oil. Knead gently.

Dough will be soft and slightly oily. Form 1-inch round balls. Flatten them somewhat in the palm of your hand and then make a slight depression in the middle with your finger, being careful not to make the dough there too thin. Put ½ teaspoon palm sugar in each depression.

With your free hand, pick up flattened piece of dough and with the fingertips of both hands, slowly push dough up and over the palm sugar. Pinch the dough together several times to seal well. Then gently roll the dough in the palm of the hands to restore its ball shape.

Put half the balls in a saucepan of boiling water and cook for about 5 minutes, or until they rise to the surface.

With a slotted spoon, carefully remove and drain on paper towels. Roll in coconut while still hot. Repeat with remaining balls. Serve at room temperature.

*Available at markets carrying Asian food products; also see *Resources* (p. 59) for mail-order sources of Indonesian foods.

MISCELLANEOUS

Coconut Milk

Coconut meat and the milk made from it are key components in Indonesian cookery. It is easy to make coconut milk from freshly grated coconut and capture the authentic taste of Indonesian dishes using it. A thick, rich milk is produced from the first squeezing of the gratings; a thinner milk is derived from a second round of squeezing.

1 COCONUT*

½ CUP WARM WATER (FOR THICK MILK)

2–3 CUPS WARM WATER (FOR THIN MILK)

Heat the coconut in a preheated oven (350°F) for 10 minutes. Cracks will form in the coconut. Remove it from the oven (with potholders!) and place in a large metal bowl on the floor. Cover the bowl with a towel and hit the coconut with a hammer to break it completely open. More than one strike may be necessary. Remove the pieces of broken coconut from the bowl. Strain the coconut water that is released through a coffee filter to remove any fibers, and set aside. Separate the coconut meat from the shell, using a dull knife to pry them apart if necessary. Remove the brown skin from the coconut meat with a vegetable peeler and grate the meat in a food processor.

To make the thick milk, put the gratings into cheesecloth or a clean white dish towel and hold the ends together. Soak the wrapped gratings in ½ cup warm water in a small bowl for a few minutes. Firmly squeeze the gratings over the bowl. About ¾ cup of thick milk will be obtained. A less efficient method of making thick coconut milk is to put the grated coconut in a sieve, wet it with warm water, and press out the milk with a spoon.

Thin milk is made by soaking the same wrapped gratings in 2–3 cups of warm water and repeating the squeezing procedure. (Use the reserved coconut water and bring the volume to 2–3 cups with warm water.)

Canned or bottled coconut milk can be purchased at specialty stores. Dishes made with it, however, will not have the authentic Indonesian taste that is provided by freshly prepared coconut milk.

*Before buying a coconut, shake it to make sure it contains water.

Shopping in Indonesia's Food Markets

Helpful Tips

The Open-Air Markets

Learning more about Indonesian food in an outdoor market setting is fascinating. These markets, or *pazar,* typically are centrally located. Some are held on a specific day of the week and are set up and dismantled the same day. Be sure to look for regional specialities. Typically, non-food items also will be available.

To get a feeling for how purchases are negotiated, stroll around the rows of food stalls and watch the lively interaction between the vendors and the local people. There can be some haggling over prices, but you will discover that the prices already are quite reasonable. Your time would be better spent saving dollars elsewhere rather than a penny or two here. If prices are not marked, however, it would be wise to see what the local folk pay so you don't end up paying a lot more.

Food in the markets is sold by the kilogram in 1/10 kilogram increments, or *ons.* To encourage sales, vendors often offer generous samples to taste. This is a good opportunity to ask for the name of an item that is not labelled. If you would like to give the Indonesian language a try, see *Helpful Phrases* (p. 63). The vendors, and many of the other Indonesians around you, will be happy to answer questions.

Some of the more unusual items in outdoor markets are exotic spices, flavorful leaves, souring agents and herbal tonics. Just a few that are generally unfamiliar to Americans are *daun pandan, andaliman, asam kandis, kluwek* and *selasih.* See *Foods & Flavors Guide* (p. 99). Ladies with herbal remedies (*jamu*) carry their wares in bottles in a big basket on their backs.

A Health Precaution

Wherever you travel, choose your food vendors with care, following the same criteria used at home. Don't ask for trouble. Some serious diseases such as dysentery, hepatitis, and cholera can be transmitted by eating unclean produce. Make sure the produce looks fresh and clean. Should there be any doubt, look for stalls that appear popular with the local people.

The Supermarkets

Be sure to shop in the large, modern supermarkets as well. They are a great place to get the makings for a tasty picnic featuring Indonesian food. Many regional specialties will tempt you. And for convenience, before leaving home, pack some lightweight tableware and a pocket knife!

The following abbreviated list of weights in Indonesian has proven sufficient to get the quantities we desired. Corresponding approximate weights in pounds are included.

100 grams: *satu ons*	⅕ pound
300 grams: *tiga ons*	⅔ pound
500 grams (half kilo): *lima ons*	1 pound

If you are considering bringing food back to the United States, check with the US Customs Service beforehand to see which items or categories of items are allowed. Ask for the latest edition of publication number 512. Changes in regulations that occurred after publication can be obtained by writing to:

Assistant Commissioner
Office of Inspection and Control
US Customs Service
Washington, DC 20229

Resources

Mail-Order Suppliers of Indonesian Food Items

Several Indonesian ingredients can be found in Asian food stores in metropolitan areas and in many university towns with large foreign student populations. One generally can find fresh root spices such as turmeric, greater galangal (laos), and ginger; fresh or frozen leaves such as Kaffir lime, *pandan, salam* and banana; bottled condiments and fish pastes; fresh lemon grass; palm sugar and candlenuts.

We have listed below some mail-order suppliers of Indonesian food items. Most have a catalog or brochure of their products and most have websites and email addresses. Please note the specific policies of each store; these can, of course, change over time. We would appreciate hearing from our readers if a listed store no longer handles mail orders. Please also bring to our attention mail-order stores of Indonesian ingredients not included here.

Bachri's
Chili & Spice Gourmet
5617 Villa Haven
Pittsburgh, PA 15236
Tel: 800-511-6451
Tel: 412-831-5452
Fax: 412-831-2542
www.lm.com/~bachris
bachris@telerama.lm.com
Check, charge or money order
No minimum order
Catalog available

Lucille and David Bigge
Spice Merchant
P.O. Box 524
Jackson Hole, WY 83001
Tel: 307-733-7811
Fax: 307-733-6343
www.emall.com/spice
71553.436@compuserve.com
Check, charge or money order
No minimum order
Catalog available

Vanns Spices Ltd.
1238 E. Joppa Rd.
Baltimore, MD 21286
Tel: 800-583-1693
Tel: 410-583-1643
Fax: 800-583-1617
Fax: 410-583-1783
vanns@pop.balt.mindspring.com
Check only
Minimum order $25.00
Product list available

Global Food Market Place
5699 Kanan Rd., Suite 333
Agoura Hills, CA 91301
Tel.: 818-706-6044
Fax: 818-879-0462
www.globalfoodmarket.com
staff@globalfoodmarket.com
Check or credit card
Minimum order $25.00
Product list available

The travel agencies listed below offer a wide variety of general and specific interest tours to Indonesia. They have been especially helpful in providing travel and culinary information for us. They do not currently market special food-related tours to Indonesia, but may do so in the future. We encourage you to inquire about their customized itineraries for independent travelers and any of their exciting tour offerings.

Absolute Asia
180 Varick St.
New York, NY 10014
Tel: 800-736-8187
Tel: 212-627-1950
Fax: 212-627-4090

Tedjo Express USA
3457 Wilshire Blvd., Suite 203
Los Angeles, CA 90010
Tel: 800-448-3356
Tel: 213-387-3838
Fax: 213-387-2968

Danu Enterprises
P.O. Box 156
Capitola, CA 95010
Tel/Fax: 888-476-0543

Bolder Adventures
Asia Transpacific Journeys
3055 Center Green Dr.
Boulder, CO 80301
Tel: 800-642-2742
Fax: 303-443-7078
www.southeastasia.com
info@southeastasia.com

Natrabu
Indo-American Travel
433 California St., Suite 630
San Francisco, CA 94104
Tel: 800-628-7228 (US)
Tel: 800-654-6900 (Calif.)
Fax: 415-362-0531

Some Useful Organizations to Know About

Indonesian Tourism Office

The Indonesian tourist promotion office for North America can assist you with your travel planning. To request travel materials or information, write or call:

Indonesian Tourist Office
3457 Wilshire Blvd.
Los Angeles, CA 90010
Tel: 213-387-2078
Tel: 213-387-8309
Fax: 213-380-4876

We are members of two international organizations that exist to promote good will and understanding between people of different cultures. Since both groups have enriched our travel experiences considerably, we would like our readers to know about them. These organizations, Servas and The Friendship Force, share similar ideals but operate somewhat differently.

Servas

Servas, from the Esperanto word meaning "serve," is a non-profit system of travelers and hosts. Servas members travel independently and make their own contacts with fellow members in other countries, choosing hosts with attributes of interest from membership rosters. It is a wonderful way to get to know people, be invited into their homes as a family member, share experiences and help promote world peace. Visits usually are for two days. Some members are available only as "day hosts," but these shorter visits, too, are rewarding. The same welcome is extended to Servas members visiting the United States. Members of Servas in the United States generally are not organized into clubs at the local or state level.

For more information about membership in Servas, write or call:

US Servas Committee, Inc.
11 John St., Suite #407
New York, NY 10038
Tel: 212-267-0252

The Friendship Force

The Friendship Force is a non-profit organization, which also fosters good will through encounters between people of different backgrounds. Unlike Servas, Friendship Force members travel in groups to host countries. Both itinerary and travel arrangements are made by a member acting as exchange director. These trips combine stays with a host family and group travel within the host country. Friendship Force members are organized on the local level, and each club is involved in several incoming and outgoing exchanges during the year.

For more information on membership in The Friendship Force, write:

The Friendship Force
Suite 575, South Tower
One CNN Center
Atlanta, GA 30303

Helpful Phrases

For Use in Restaurants and Food Markets

In the Restaurant

The following phrases in Indonesian will assist you in ordering food, learning more about the dish you ordered, and determining what specialties of a region are available. Each phrase also is written phonetically to help with pronunciation. Syllables in capital letters are accented. Letters in parentheses are essentially soundless.

DO YOU HAVE A MENU?	Apakah ada daftar makanan / menu? *AH-pah-kah AH-dah DAHF-tahr mah-KAH-nahn / MEH-noo?*
MAY I SEE THE MENU, PLEASE?	Minta lihat daftar makanan / menunya? *MIN-tah LEE-haht DAHF-tahr mah-KAH-nahn / meh-NOO-nyah?*
WHAT DO YOU RECOMMEND?	Masakan apa saja yang anda sarankan? *Mah-SAH-kahn AH-pah SIGH-jah young AHN-dah sah-RAHN-kahn?*
DO YOU HAVE . . . HERE? (ADD AN ITEM FROM THE MENU GUIDE OR THE FOODS & FLAVORS GUIDE.)	Apakah ada . . . di sini? *AH-pah-kah AH-dah . . . dee SEE-nee?*

63

Helpful Phrases

ARE THERE ANY "SPECIALS" TODAY?

Apakah ada masakan istimewa hari ini?

AH-pah-kah AH-dah mah-SAH-kahn is-tee-MAY-wah HAH-ree IN-nee?

DO YOU HAVE ANY SPECIAL REGIONAL DISHES?

Apakah ada masakan khas daerah ini?

AH-pah-kah AH-dah mah-SAH-kahn (k)hahs DIE-rah IN-nee?

IS THIS DISH SPICY?

Masakan ini, apakah pedas?

Mah-SAH-kahn IN-nee, AH-pah-kah PEH-dahs?

I / WE WOULD LIKE TO ORDER . . .

Saya / kami mau pesan . . .

SIGH-yah / KAH-mee mau PEH-sun . . .

WHAT ARE THE INGREDIENTS IN THIS DISH?

Bahan bahan apa yang dipakai dalam masakan ini?

BAH-hahn BAH-hahn AH-pah young dee-PAH-kay DAH-lahm mah-SAH-kahn IN-nee?

WHAT ARE THE SEASONINGS IN THIS DISH?

Bumbu bumbu apa yang dipakai dalam masakan ini?

BOOM-boo BOOM-boo AH-pah young dee-PAH-kay DAH-lahm mah-SAH-kahn IN-nee?

THANK YOU VERY MUCH. THE FOOD WAS DELICIOUS.

Terima kasih banyak. Masakannya enak sekali.

Teh-REE-mah KAH-see BAH-nyah(k). Mah-sah-KAHN-nyah EH-nah(k) seh-KAH-lee.

In the Market

The following phrases will help you make purchases and learn more about unfamiliar produce, spices and herbs.

WHAT ARE THE REGIONAL FRUITS AND VEGETABLES?

Buah buahan dan sayur sayuran apa saja yang khas di daerah ini?

BOO-ah boo-AH-hahn dahn SIGH-yer sigh-YER-ahn AH-pah SAH-jah young (k)hahs dee DIE-rah IN-nee?

WHAT IS THIS CALLED?

Ini apa namanya?

IN-nee AH-pah nah-MAH-nyah?

DO YOU HAVE . . . HERE? (ADD AN ITEM FROM THE *FOODS & FLAVORS GUIDE*.)

Apakah ada . . . di sini?

AH-pah-kah AH-dah . . . dee SEE-nee?

MAY I TASTE THIS?

Boleh saya cicipi ini?

BOH-lay SIGH-yah chee-CHEE-pee IN-nee?

WHERE CAN I BUY FRESH . . . ?

Di mana saya dapat beli . . . yang segar?

Dee MAH-nah SIGH-yah DAH-paht BEH-lee . . . young SEH-gahr?

HOW MUCH IS THIS PER KILOGRAM?

Ini, berapa harganya sekilo?

IN-nee, beh-RAH-pah har-GAH-nyah seh-KEE-loh?

I WOULD LIKE TO BUY . . . 1/10 KILOGRAM OF THIS / THAT.

Saya mau beli ini / itu . . . ons.

SIGH-yah mau BEH-lee IN nee / E-too . . . ownce.

MAY I PHOTOGRAPH THIS?

Boleh saya memotret ini?

BOH-leh SIGH-yah meh-MOH-treht I(N)-nee?

Other Useful Phrases

Sometimes it helps to see in writing a word or phrase that is said to you in Indonesian, because certain letters have distinctly different sounds in Indonesian than in English. You may be familiar with the word and its English translation but less familiar with its pronunciation. The following phrase comes in handy if you want to see the word or phrase you are hearing.

PLEASE WRITE IT ON A PIECE OF PAPER.	Tolong tuliskan itu di kertas. *TOH-long too-LEES-kahn E-too dee CUR-tahs.*

Interested in bringing home books about Indonesian food? Perhaps someone knows just the place for you to look, if you pose the following question:

WHERE CAN I BUY AN INDONESIAN COOKBOOK IN ENGLISH?	Di mana saya bisa beli buku masakan Indonesia yang ditulis dalam bahasa Inggeris? *Dee MAH-nah SIGH-yah BEE-sah BEH-lee BOO-koo mah-SAH-kahn In-doh-NEIGH-see-ah young dee-TOO-lees DAH-lahm bah-HAH-sah ING-grees?*

And, of course, the following phrases also are useful to know.

WHERE IS THE LADIES' / MEN'S RESTROOM?	Di mana kamar kecilnya? *Dee MAH-nah KAH-mahr keh-CHEEL-nyah?*
WAITER / WAITRESS, I / WE ARE DONE. MAY I / WE HAVE THE CHECK, PLEASE?	Mas (male waiter) / Mbak (female waitress), sudah. Minta bonnya? *Mahs / EHM-bahk, SOO-dah. MIN-tah BOHN-nya?*
DO YOU ACCEPT CREDIT CARDS? TRAVELERS CHECKS?	Apakah bisa bayar pakai kartu credit? traveler cek? *AH-pah-kah BEE-sah BUY-yar PAH-kay KAR-too KREH-dit? TRAVE-ler chehk?*

Menu Guide

This alphabetical listing is an extensive compilation of menu entries in Indonesian, with English translations, to make ordering food easy. It includes typical Indonesian dishes as well as specialties characteristic of the different regions of the archipelago.

Classic regional dishes of Indonesia that should not be missed are labeled "regional classic" in the margin next to the menu entry. Note that outside a particular geographical area, these specialties rarely are available unless a restaurant features one or more regional cuisines. Some noteworthy dishes popular throughout much of the archipelago—also not to be missed—are labeled "national favorite." Comments on some of our favorites also are included in the margin.

With *Eat Smart in Indonesia* in hand, you will quickly become more familiar with restaurant cuisine. Be sure to take it to breakfast in the hotel; there will be plenty of items to identify. Breakfast, or *makan pagi,* is available early in the day. Try some of the wonderful breakfast porridges (*bubur*) and delicious fresh fruit. You will be astounded at the number of unfamiliar ones to sample. Be daring, and try the *durian!* Lunch, or *makan siang,* typically consists of rice with an assortment of meat and vegetable dishes. Tea or coffee will accompany the meal. The Indonesians make some of the most creative and delicious drinks, combining fruits, coconut milk, palm sugar, droplets of colored rice or sago flour and several unusual flavorings. *Es cendol,* or *es dawet,* as it is called in some areas, is a favorite. As always when traveling, it is wise to drink bottled rather than tap water. Dinner, or *makan malam,* is the main meal of the day. Like lunch, it also includes rice and several meat and vegetable dishes. It is enjoyed in the early evening when the temperature is cooler. This is also a good time to check out night food stalls, which suddenly appear on sidewalks used as busy daytime walkways.

Be aware that eateries in many parts of the country don't open until after sunset during Puasa, the Muslim, month-long fasting period. The date changes each year according to the Islamic lunar calendar. Chinese restaurants, however, will be open during this holiday.

abon shredded, boiled meat seasoned and fried until crispy. It is a popular side dish or garnish for preparations such as *nasi rames* or *nasi rawon*. Softer-textured meat, fried briefly and sweetened with palm sugar, is used as a filling for rice rolls steamed in banana leaves (see *lemper,* this Guide).

NATIONAL FAVORITE **acar** a condiment of cucumbers and other vegetables, especially carrots, in a sweet and sour sauce of sugary vinegar.

acar babi pickled pork.

acar bawang pickled onions.

acar campur mixed pickles.

acar ikan pickled fish.

acar jagung corn pickles.

acar ketimun cucumber pickles.

acar lobak white radish relish.

acar lombok hijau pickled green chili peppers.

acar nanas pickled pineapples.

air jeruk orange juice.

Ambon see *bika Ambon.*

ame kemute hard-boiled eggs, flattened and simmered in coconut-based sweet and sour sauce.

REGIONAL CLASSIC **ampiang dadiah** a dish of buffalo yogurt, palm sugar, grated coconut and sticky (glutinous) rice that has been fried, flattened and dried. This specialty of Bukittinggi, West Sumatra, is popular for breakfast or dessert. Also called *dadiah campur.*

amplang kuku macan crescent-shaped snacks flavored with fish, a specialty of East Kalimantan.

REGIONAL CLASSIC **angsli** a warm dessert made of coconut milk, bread cubes, roasted peanuts, colorful bits of dried tapioca (*pacar* Cina) and small squares of cake formed of extruded sticky (glutinous) rice-flour dough (*petulo*). It is a specialty of Malang, East Java.

anyang sarden a relish of sardines, onions and chili peppers.

anyang tauge dan pakis a salad of bean sprouts and fiddleheads.

anyang telur terubok a relish made from shad roe.

DELICIOUS **apem** a molded pancake made of rice or tapioca flour filled with nuts or coconut, served with a sauce of coconut milk sweetened with palm sugar and flavored with leaves called *daun pandan.*

arem arem a dish from Malang, East Java, containing tempe, bean sprouts and chunks of compressed, sticky (glutinous) rice. It is covered with sweet soy sauce and coconut water, and topped with chopped peanuts and grated coconut.

ares young banana tree stalks, chopped and boiled in duck stock.

ares ayam a mixture of chicken with chopped, boiled stalks of young banana plants.

arsik a North Sumatran ceremonial dish of fried goldfish (carp) stuffed with bamboo shoots or with long green beans. The stuffing typically is flavored with wild pepper, or *andaliman,* a lemony spice that slightly numbs the mouth. To prevent the fish from burning and also impart additional flavor to the dish, lemon grass and the stems of the pineapple-like fruit called *asam kincung* are placed beneath the fish in the frying pan. **REGIONAL FAVORITE**

asam asam spicy, steamed chicken giblets in coconut milk, a specialty of East Java. It is made sour by the addition of sour fruits such as tamarind, *belimbing wuluh* or *asam kandis.* A Central Javanese version includes *kilkil,* the tendons and cartilage of cattle hooves.

asam babi goreng fried pork with tamarind.

asam manis sweet and sour beef grilled on skewers.

asinan a mixture of fresh, crunchy fruits and vegetables in a hot (spicy) sweet and sour sauce with peanuts. It is a specialty of Bogor, West Java. **REGIONAL CLASSIC**

ayam bakar grilled chicken.

ayam bakar bumbu cabe grilled chicken with chili pepper sauce.

ayam bakar kecap grilled chicken with sweet soy sauce.

ayam bakar rica grilled chicken with hot chili peppers. It is a specialty of Manado, North Sulawesi. **SPICY**

ayam balado browned chicken in hot chili pepper sauce, a local dish of Bukittinggi, West Sumatra. **SPICY**

ayam bawang chicken with onions.

ayam besengek chicken cooked in a special spice paste called *bumbu besengek,* which typically includes shallots, garlic, candlenuts, hot red chili peppers, coriander, turmeric, laos, shrimp paste and lemon grass, in coconut milk. **IRRESTISTIBLE**

ayam betutu whole, dressed chicken stuffed with a spice paste, and grilled or slow-cooked underground for 6–8 hours in hot embers. When cooked underground, the chicken is wrapped in palm leaves, covered with rice hulls and placed inside a ceramic bowl. It is a special Balinese dish. **REGIONAL CLASSIC**

ayam bumbu rujak chicken cooked in spicy coconut-based hot and sour sauce containing chili peppers, palm sugar, tamarind water and shrimp paste.

ayam goreng crispy fried chicken. **TASTY**

ayam goreng asam piquant fried chicken.

ayam goreng Jawa Javanese-style fried chicken. Chicken pieces are cooked in spicy, coconut milk-based sauce until they absorb the sauce, and then are deep-fried.

FABULOUS **ayam goreng Kalasan** chicken simmered in coconut water and then deep-fried. It is a specialty of Kalasan, Central Java. It is also called *ayam* mBok Berek after mBok (Mrs.) Berek, who created the dish.

EXCELLENT CHOICE **ayam gulai** chicken curry.

ayam guling chicken roasted on a revolving spit.

ayam kampung panggang Klaten free-running chicken prepared in the style of Klaten, Central Java. Chicken pieces are cooked in a spicy, coconut-based sauce containing ground candlenuts. After the sauce is reduced, the meat is roasted until crispy.

ayam kodok stuffed, boneless chicken shaped like a frog. To make this dish, the meat and bones are laboriously removed from the skin to minimize tearing. The meat is removed from the bones, minced and seasoned, and stuffed back into the intact skin, which is then sewn shut. With gentle flattening, the stuffed skin looks like a frog. It is steamed and then roasted until crispy.

ayam kuah chicken in broth.

ayam kuah jeruk chicken in orange sauce.

ayam kukus isi braised, stuffed chicken.

ayam laksa chicken with cellophane noodles.

REGIONAL CLASSIC **ayam masak dibulu** Minahasan-style (North Sulawesi) chicken cooked in sections of green bamboo.

ayam mBok Berek see *ayam goreng* Kalasan.

ayam panggang roasted chicken.

DELICIOUS **ayam panggang bumbu rujak** roasted chicken in a spicy coconut-based hot and sour sauce containing chili peppers, tamarind water, palm sugar and shrimp paste.

ayam panggang kecap roasted chicken with soy sauce.

ayam panggang pedas spicy (hot) roasted chicken.

TASTY **ayam pecel** fried chicken served with a mixed salad of blanched vegetables and spicy (hot) peanut sauce.

ayam petis chicken with fish or shrimp sauce.

ayam pop light-colored chicken that has been boiled, then lightly fried in a little oil. It is not dark and crispy like *ayam goreng*.

ayam sambal bawang chicken cooked with red chili peppers and shallots.

REGIONAL CLASSIC **ayam Taliwang** grilled, butterflied chicken, a specialty of Lombok.

ayam tuturuga curried chicken, a special preparation of Manado, North Sulawesi.

ayam woku a casserole of chicken cooked in a paste of chili peppers, ginger, garlic and shallots mixed with chopped leeks. It is a specialty of Sulawesi.

EXCELLENT CHOICE

babat goreng fried beef tripe.

babat goreng asam pedas sweet and sour fried beef tripe.

babi bumbu Cina spicy pork stew, a Chinese-inspired dish. Unlike Muslim Indonesians, the Chinese are not prohibited from eating pork because of religious beliefs.

babi goreng tomat fried pork with tomatoes.

babi gulai pork curry.

babi guling roast suckling pig, Bali's most famous dish. Not all roasted pigs, however, are piglets. The dressed animal is stuffed with a spice paste containing candlenuts, hot chili peppers, lemon grass, coriander, ginger, shallots and shrimp paste and then sewed shut. It is spit-roasted over hot coals of dried coconut husks. The skin, the favorite part of the pig, is basted with turmeric in oil, making it golden-colored and crispy. In North Sulawesi, the dish is called *babi putar,* and is served with a sauce called *dabu dabu,* which is made with chopped chili peppers, shallots and tomatoes, seasoned with lime and a paste of fermented fish intestines called *bakasang.*

REGIONAL CLASSIC

babi kecap pork with soy sauce.

babi kucai pork with leeks or chives.

babi masak lobak pork with daikon radish.

babi panggang roast pork with rice and blood sauce, a specialty of the Karonese, a group of Batak people in North Sumatra, near the city of Berastagi.

REGIONAL CLASSIC

babi putar see *babi guling.*

bagar kambing goat curry.

bagea a brittle cake made of sago flour and *kanari* nuts. It is a specialty of the islands of North Maluku.

bajigur a hot drink made of coconut milk, coffee and spices. It is a West Javanese specialty.

DELICIOUS

bakar ikan barbecued fish.

bakmi (bakmie) goreng stir-fried egg noddles with bits of vegetables, and sometimes meat or shrimp. This dish is also called *mi (mie) goreng.*

NATIONAL FAVORITE

bakmi udang noodles with shrimp.

bakpao a steamed bun stuffed with meat or other ingredients.

bakpia a sweetmeat of dough filled with a mixture of mung beans and cane sugar. It is a specialty of Yogyakarta, Central Java.

NATIONAL FAVORITE **bakso (baso, ba'so)** meatballs, or a soup with meatballs. It is a popular street food.

bakso ayam goreng fried meatballs made with chicken.

bakso Lapangan Tembak beefball soup made according to the recipe of the *warung,* or outdoor food stall, famous for it, located near the firing range (Lapangan Tembak) at the Senayan Sports Center in Jakarta.

REGIONAL CLASSIC **bakso tahu goreng** fried tofu stuffed with meat paste, and topped with peanut sauce. It is a specialty of Bandung, West Java.

bakwan a deep-fried meat or corn fritter, or a meatball soup.

bakwan jagung a deep-fried corn fritter; also called *perkedel jagung* and *bregedel.*

bakwan jagung dengan udang corn fritters with shrimp.

bakwan tauge bean sprout fritters.

bandeng isi stuffed milkfish. The flesh and bones are removed through the gills or mouth, without ripping the skin. The flesh, mixed with various spices, is cooked and then stuffed back into the skin.

WONDERFUL **bandrek** a West Javanese hot drink made with coconut milk, grated coconut, ginger, palm sugar and black pepper.

baso (ba'so) see *bakso.*

REGIONAL CLASSIC **bebek betutu** a special Balinese dish of whole, dressed duck stuffed with a spice paste, and grilled or slow-cooked underground in hot embers. When cooked underground, the duck is wrapped in palm leaves, covered with rice hulls and placed inside a ceramic bowl.

bebotok ayam minced chicken with spices, wrapped in banana leaves and steamed.

bebotok udang shrimp with spices, wrapped in banana leaves and steamed.

besengek ayam kampung free-range chicken, barbecued and then cooked in a spicy sauce consisting of shallots, garlic, candlenuts, hot red chili peppers, coriander, turmeric, laos, shrimp paste, and lemon grass, in coconut milk.

NATIONAL FAVORITE **bihun** thin rice noodles or a dish made with these noodles and vegetables.

bihun baso rice noodles, vegetables and small balls of fish or meat.

bihun goreng thin rice noodles fried with bits of vegetables and meat or seafood.

bihun kangkung udang thin rice noodles, shrimp, water spinach and bits of other vegetables.

bihun kuah a soup containing thin rice noodles.

bika (bikang) a yellow, "plug-shaped" sweetmeat having a gelatin-like consistency, made with eggs, rice flour and sugar. It often is individually wrapped in cellophane.

bika Ambon a yellow rice-flour cake containing jackfruit; sometimes simply called Ambon.

bikang coklat a chocolate rice-flour cake.

bipang a sweet cake made of puffed rice.

bistek daging braised beefsteak.

bolang baling a puffy, fried yeast doughnut; it is a specialty of Semarang, Central Java.

bolu mekar see *kue mangkuk.*

botok a Central Javanese dish made with shrimp, vegetables, spices and grated coconut, and steamed in banana leaves.

bregedel see *bakwan jagung.*

brongkos daging a meat stew flavored and colored with *kluwek,* the black, pasty material in the nuts of the *kepayang* tree. It is a specialty of Yogyakarta in Central Java.

buah jingah sweet potato fritters, a specialty of the Banjar people of South Kalimantan; called *tai kuda* in North Sulawesi.

bubur ayam a traditional breakfast dish of rice porridge with chicken. The porridge is sprinkled with bits of chicken, fried shallots, celery leaves and thin slices of *cakwe,* a long, light fritter. Steaming hot, spicy chicken soup is then poured on top.

bubur cenil a dessert specialty of Surabaya, East Java, and the island of Madura, served in a banana leaf. It contains coconut milk, beads and chunks of colored sago flour dough and bits of cake made with rice flour, topped with palm sugar.

bubur hitam a porridge made with black rice; also called *bubur injin.*

bubur ikan fish porridge.

bubur injin see *bubur hitam.*

bubur kacang hijau a porridge made with mung beans.

bubur kacang tanah a sweet, loose porridge made with unroasted peanuts. Also called *wedang kacang putih.*

bubur Manado a bright-yellow porridge made primarily of vegetables. It contains corn, manioc (cassava), pumpkin, spinach and rice. Seasonings include fish paste and chili peppers. It is a specialty of Manado, northern Sulawesi. Also called *tinutuan.*

bugis small, sticky (glutinous) rice-flour cakes filled with coconut and palm sugar, and steamed in banana leaves.

bulat steamed fishballs made with the same mixture of sago flour and knifefish (*belida*) used to make the dish called *empek empek* (this Guide).

bumbu sate see *sambal kacang.*

INTERESTING **buntil** a mixture of dried anchovy fry, coconut meat and chopped broad beans called *pete,* wrapped in manioc (cassava) leaves and steamed in a banana leaf. The *sambal,* or condiment, served with this Javanese specialty contains flowers from the fruit called *asam kincung* (see *Food & Flavors Guide*).

buras a rice cake cooked in thick coconut milk, wrapped in banana leaves and steamed. These cakes can be filled with a mixture of chopped meat and vegetables.

REGIONAL CLASSIC **burung dara goreng** deep-fried dove, a specialty of Yogyakarta, Central Java.

NATIONAL FAVORITE **cap cai (cap cay, cap coy)** a stir-fried dish of chopped, mixed vegetables, meat and fish.

cingur see *rujak cingur.*

cipera chicken soup made with corn flour, coconut milk and spices.

cis pleng a salad of fresh chopped vegetables with peanut sauce.

colenak grilled fermented manioc (cassava), covered with a sauce of grated coconut and palm sugar.

REGIONAL CLASSIC **colo colo** an Ambonese (Maluku Islands) sweet and sour sauce for fish, made with chili peppers and citrus fruits.

combro hot (spicy) snack foods such as fried, mashed manioc (cassava) filled with *oncom,* the residue from peanuts or coconut after the oil has been extracted, with hot chili pepper sauce.

coto (soto) Makassar campur beef tripe soup, a specialty of Ujung Pandang (formerly Makassar), South Sulawesi.

REGIONAL CLASSIC **coto (soto) Makassar daging** a meaty soup-like dish with broth mixed with a spice paste and freshly ground peanuts. It traditionally is served with a rice cake called *buras.* This dish is a specialty of Ujung Pandang (formerly Makassar), South Sulawesi.

cucur a fried cake made of rice flour.

cumi cumi hitam squid cooked in sauce containing their ink.

dabu dabu a raw vegetable salad of chopped tomatoes, chili   REGIONAL CLASSIC
peppers, shallots, Javanese almonds and sometimes fermented
fish paste. It is a specialty of Ambon (Maluku Islands). In
North Sulawesi it is the name of a *sambal,* or condiment, with
chili peppers and fermented fish paste, which is served with
whole, roast pig or grilled fish.

dadar omelette.

dadar isi udang an omelette filled with shrimp.

dadar kepiting a crabmeat omelette, a treat of Sidoarjo, East Java.   GOOD CHOICE

dadar lombok chili pepper omelette.

dadar nasi rice omelette.

dadar telur kentang potato omelette.

dadiah campur see *ampiang dadiah.*

daging gulung a roulade of meat.

daging se'i smoked beef, a specialty of Timor.

dawet see *es dawet.*

dendeng slices of meat coated with a spicy paste and sun-dried. It
is fried before serving.

dendeng balado spicy, sun-dried meat fried with red chili   SPICY
peppers, shallots, lime leaves, and lemon grass. It is a specialty
of the Minangkabau people of Padang, West Sumatra.

dendeng paru dried, fried beef lung; also called *dendeng rabu.*

dendeng rabu see *dendeng paru.*

dendeng ragi meat cooked with spices and grated coconut until dry.   DELICIOUS

dodol soft fudge made of sticky (glutinous) rice, coconut milk,
palm sugar and sometimes the fruit called *durian.* It is a
specialty of Perbaungan, North Sumatra.

dodol Garut hard cakes of fudge. This specialty of Garut, West
Java, is made of sticky (glutinous) rice, coconut milk and palm
sugar and is harder than the *dodol* made in North Sumatra.

donat sate a chocolate-coated yeast doughnut served on a skewer.

empal cubes of marinated meat that have been boiled, pounded
flat and then fried.

empal gankik *empal* made with beef shoulder meat.

Menu Guide

REGIONAL CLASSIC empal gentong *empal* cooked in an earthenware pot and served with a condiment of dried, powdered chili peppers. It is a specialty of Cirebon, West Java.

empal jantung *empal* made with pieces of heart.

empal Jawa Javanese-style *empal* made of beef marinated in sweet soy sauce and chili peppers.

WONDERFUL empek empek a fish cake made of sago flour and minced fish, served on cellophane noodles and covered with a sauce of chili peppers, garlic, dried shrimp, palm sugar, soy sauce and vinegar. This specialty of Palembang, South Sumatra, is made with a popular local fish called *ikan belida,* a knifefish. The dish is also called *pempek (pe empek), lenjeran* and *panjang.* Preparations of fish cakes stuffed with a whole, hard-boiled egg are called *pempek telur, pempek kapal selam* or *kapal selam.* This sago flour and mashed fish mixture is quite versatile; formed into different shapes, it becomes a key ingredient in some other regional specialties of Palembang (see *bulat, model, sate ikan belida* and *tekwan,* this Guide).

EXTRAORDINARY es alpokat (advokat) an avocado and chocolate shake. Also called *es pokat.*

es buah an iced drink containing several fruits including *kolang kaling,* or sugar palm fruit, coconut milk and red-colored syrup, or *stroop.*

es campur an iced fruit drink with sugar syrup and small blobs of colored rice-flour dough called *cendol.*

ASTOUNDING es cendol (cindol) a refreshing drink made of palm sugar, coconut milk and small blobs of green-colored rice flour dough. It is served with palm sugar on the bottom, coconut milk on top and dough pieces floating in the middle. The ingredients are mixed before drinking. In some parts of the country it is called *es dawet.*

es cincau a drink using green gelatin from leaves called *daun cincau.*

es dawet see *es cendol.*

es doger coconut milk sorbet with rose-flavored syrup, fermented manioc (cassava) and bits of dried, multicolored tapioca called *pacar* Cina.

es jeruk iced orange juice.

es jus iced fruit juice.

es kelapa muda an iced drink made with unripe coconut meat.

NATIONAL FAVORITE es kopyor an iced drink made with syrup and developmentally different coconuts, whose meat remains soft and blended with their water.

es krim apokat avocado ice cream.

es pallubutung an iced drink made with bananas in a thick, creamy sauce containing coconut and rice. It is a specialty of Ujung Pandang, South Sulawesi. REGIONAL CLASSIC

es pokat see *es alpokat.*

es puter hand-turned coconut milk sorbet made the traditional way by using crushed ice and salt to freeze it.

es selasih an iced drink made with mixed fruit and coconut water. Seeds from a basil variety having purplish stems provide its characteristic flavor. Before use, dried seeds are placed in hot water, which causes them to swell and become gelatinous on the surface. Also called *es telasih.* UNUSUAL

es stroop (es setrop) an iced drink made with syrup; it is a Javanese specialty.

es tape (es tapai) an iced drink made with fermented, black, sticky (glutinous) rice, sometimes topped with vanilla-flavored syrup. WONDERFUL

es tebak an iced drink made with fruit, sticky (glutinous) rice and *cendol,* blobs of green-colored rice flour.

es teh iced tea.

es telasih see *es selasih.*

es teler a dish of mixed fruits, grated young (green) coconuts, colored chunks of agar, cubes and droplets made of sago-flour dough, topped with condensed milk and ice shavings. GREAT

feng a dish of Portuguese origin made with pork giblets.

frikadel daging kecil an appetizer or snack of small meatballs.

frikadel kepiting kecil an appetizer or snack of small balls of crabmeat.

frikadel tahu dengan udang an appetizer or snack of small balls of shrimp and tofu.

gado gado a salad of blanched or steamed vegetables topped with a sauce made with spices and ground peanuts. FLAVORFUL

gampol plered a sweet snack made with rice flour, coconut milk and spices; it is a specialty of Surakarta (Solo), Central Java. REGIONAL CLASSIC

gandos a cookie made of rice flour and coconut.

gedang mekuah papaya soup.

gemblong a crunchy fried ball of sticky (glutinous) rice carmelized with palm sugar. It is a treat of North Sulawesi and West Java.

REGIONAL CLASSIC **geplak** a sweet cake made of sticky (glutinous) rice, cane sugar and grated coconut. This specialty of Yogyakarta, Central Java, is available in several different shapes.

gepok pukul Cianjur cooked beef, pounded and shredded, then fried and tied together with bamboo. It is a specialty of Cianjur, West Java.

INTERESTING **getuk lindri** a cake made of puréed sweet potato or manioc (cassava), coconut milk and palm sugar. The mixture, often colored, is extruded through a ricer, producing strands that are formed into round or loaf cakes and topped with grated coconut.

gimbal tahu Semarang chunks of tofu deep-fried in tempura-like batter and served with sweet soy sauce. It is a specialty of Semarang, Central Java.

FABULOUS **gimbal udang** a shrimp fritter.

gohu a salad of unripe papaya in fermented bonito fish sauce, called *bakasang,* and lime. It is a specialty of North Sulawesi.

goreng babat fried tripe.

goreng hati fried liver.

goreng ikan dengan kuah tomat fried fish in tomato sauce.

goreng sambal lada hijau a *sambal,* or condiment, made of fried green chili peppers.

goreng tahu dengan sambal kecap fried tofu with soy sauce.

goreng terong fried eggplant.

growol a mixture of grated coconut and manioc (cassava) served in a banana leaf.

gudangan steamed mixed vegetables with grated coconut and chili peppers.

REGIONAL CLASSIC **gudeg** a combination plate of unripe jackfruit cooked in coconut milk, chicken cooked in a spicy, coconut-based sauce, rice, a piece of buffalo skin that has been processed into a cracker snack and a dollop of coconut cream sauce. *Gudeg* dishes are a specialty of Yogyakarta, Central Java.

gudeg kendil *gudeg* that is cooked in an earthenware pot as "take-away" food.

gudeg telur tahu *gudeg* with tofu and a hard-boiled egg.

EXCELLENT **gulai ayam** curried chicken stew.

gulai babat curried tripe stew.

gulai bagar curried goat.

gulai buncis curried green beans.

gulai cubadak curried jackfruit stew.

gulai gajebo curried beef brisket.   GREAT

gulai ikan kakap curried snapper.

gulai kambing kecap curried goat or lamb stew with soy sauce.

gulai otak curried brains with aromatic leaves called *daun mangkuk*.

gulai pareh a spicy (hot) curry of meat or fish.

gulai tunjang curried stew of buffalo trotters.

gule sumsum curried stew of goat shanks with marrow.

hati ampla gulung a roulade of liver and gizzards.

hati ayam asam manis sweet and sour chicken livers.

ikan arsip rolled fish fillets.

ikan bakar grilled fish.

ikan baronang bakar grilled fish called *baronang*, a large seawater   REGIONAL CLASSIC
fish prized in South Sulawesi.

ikan bumbu santen fried fish with spicy coconut milk.

ikan bungkus a mixture of fish and spices rolled in cabbage
leaves and baked.

ikan goreng fried fish.

ikan goreng ketumbar fish marinated in coriander and lime juice,
and fried.

ikan gurami tauco gurami fish in fermented soybean sauce.

ikan kacang tanah fish with peanut sauce.

ikan mas panggang roasted goldfish.   SCRUMPTIOUS

ikan pepes fish covered with a paste of spices, wrapped in a
banana leaf and steamed.

ikan pindang fish cooked in water with spices.

ikan rica rica fish cooked in a spicy (hot) chili pepper paste; it is   SPICY
a specialty of the Minahasan people of North Sulawesi.

ikan salai smoked fish, a specialty of Pekanbaru, West Sumatra.

ikan semur Jawa Javanese-style braised fish in sweet soy sauce.

ikan tim steamed fish.

ikan woku fish rubbed with a paste of candlenuts, ginger and   REGIONAL CLASSIC
chili peppers mixed with chopped tomato, turmeric, mint and

green onion, and then wrapped in a banana leaf and grilled. It is a specialty of Sulawesi.

itik bumbu santen duck cooked in a spicy (hot) coconut sauce.

REGIONAL CLASSIC **itik panggang Banjar** roast duck; it is a specialty of the Banjar people of South Kalimantan.

jada manten a cookie or cake made of sticky (glutinous) rice.

jagung panggang grilled corn on the cob.

jahe telur a hot drink of fresh beaten eggs in sweetened ginger-flavored water.

WONDERFUL **jajan** a pink or light-green pancake made of rice flour and filled with fruit and grated coconut. In Java, *jajan* means "snacking."

jangan asam daging a sour vegetable soup with meat. It is a specialty of Kalimantan.

jemblem fried, mashed sweet potatoes with a palm sugar filling.

jenang gula taffy made of sticky (glutinous) rice, coconut and palm sugar.

EXCELLENT **jukut urap** a mixture of blanched, chopped vegetables, especially string beans and starfruit leaves, mixed with spices and grated coconut. It is the Balinese version of *urap* (see this *Guide*).

kacang goreng fried peanuts.

kacang padi sweet porridges; those made with mung beans are typical.

kakap bumbu acar sea perch with turmeric-flavored pickled carrots and cucumbers.

REGIONAL CLASSIC **kalio** meat cooked in coconut milk and spices until the sauce is partially reduced. It is a traditional dish made by the Minangkabau people in West Sumatra. Also spelled *klio*.

kalio kulit a *kalio* with buffalo or beef skin.

kalio paku a *kalio* of fiddleheads.

kambing bakar bumbu spicy barbecued goat or lamb.

REGIONAL CLASSIC **kampiun** a popular West Sumatran breakfast made by combining a sweet porridge called *kacang padi* and a fruit compote called *kolak* (see *Foods & Flavors Guide*).

kapal selam see *empek empek*.

karas karas a fried cookie made with wheat flour.

kare ayam chicken curry.

TOP A refreshingly cool welcome drink of coconut water at the Indra Palace, Bandar Lampung, southern Sumatra. **BOTTOM LEFT** Friendly vegetable sellers in the market in Solo (Surakarta), central Java. **BOTTOM RIGHT** A young girl in the market in Malang, eastern Java, looking for the right clay mortar (*cobek*) and pestle (*ulek ulek*) to make spice pastes.

TOP LEFT Hot foods from the grill (*sate panas*) neatly displayed in a *warung* in Solo (Surakarta), central Java. **TOP RIGHT** A selection of dishes comprising *nasi* Kapau at Uni Lis, a *warung* in the upper market (*Pasar Atas*) in Bukittinggi, western Sumatra. These meat and vegetable dishes are a specialty of the nearby village of Kapau. **BOTTOM** Roasted goldfish (*ikan mas panggang*) served at the Rumba Homestay, Tuk Tuk, Lake Toba, northern Sumatra.

TOP Indonesian classics made by Chef Suardana at the Puri Bagus Villa, Candidasa, Bali: left, *gado gado,* a vegetable salad topped with peanut sauce; right, *nasi campur,* a combination plate of eggs, meat or fish, vegetables and rice, topped with a sauce. **MIDDLE** Sliced *pepes ikan belida,* a paste of sago flour and mashed knifefish (*belida*), shaped into a roll and steamed in a banana leaf, a savory specialty at the Rumah Makan Selera Indonesia, Bandar Lampung, southern Sumatra. **BOTTOM** *Jajan pasar,* a dish of assorted traditional cakes served at the Indra Palace, Bandar Lampung, southern Sumatra.

TOP LEFT A vendor in Bandung, western Java, selling popular salads of assorted tart fruits topped with *rujak,* a spicy sauce made with with fermented shrimp paste, tamarind, palm sugar and chili peppers. **TOP RIGHT** Making *tinombur* at the Rumba Homestay, Tuk Tuk, Lake Toba, northern Sumatra. This condiment, a favorite of the Bakak people, contains *andaliman,* or jungle pepper. **BOTTOM** Selling bananas and pieces of the enormous jackfruit in Besakih, eastern Bali.

TOP LEFT Sweet and savory treats and the makings for a warm, soup-like dessert called *angsli*, a tasty specialty of Malang, eastern Java, served at the Tugu Park Hotel. **TOP RIGHT** Tempe made in banana leaves for sale at the outdoor market in Bukittinggi, western Sumatra. **BOTTOM LEFT** *Es cendol*, a delicious and refreshing cold drink made with palm sugar, coconut milk and droplets of green rice-flour dough (*cendol*), attractively served at the Rumah Makan Selera Indonesia, Bandar Lampung, southern Sumatra. **BOTTOM RIGHT** Food cooking in bamboo sections, Manado, northern Sulawesi.

TOP LEFT Mounds of chili peppers and other vegetables in the market in Yogyakarta, central Java. **TOP RIGHT** *Kolang kaling,* the jelly-like fruits of the *aren* palm in colorful plastic buckets at the market in Solo (Surakarta), central Java. **BOTTOM** Buffalo milk yogurt made in green bamboo sections, tempting buyers at the market in Tomohon, northern Sulawesi.

TOP Balinese specialties made by Gusti Nyoman Darte at Cucu Warung in Ubud, Bali: left, *tum hati ayam*, spicy minced chicken livers steamed in banana leaves; right, *sate* Bali *limbat*, minced meat grilled on skewers. A basket of cooking ingredients is in the background. **TOP LEFT** *Rambutan*, a red fruit with hair-like projections and tart flesh that tastes like litchi nuts, at the outdoor market in Tomohon, northern Sulawesi. **BOTTOM LEFT** A festive display of desserts made by Chef Dewa Pastika, Keraton Bali Hotel, Jimbaran, Bali. **RIGHT** Delicious palm sugar artistically wrapped in palm leaves, at the outdoor market, Tomohon, northern Sulawesi.

TOP LEFT Selling vegetables from a bicycle in Metro, southern Sumatra. **TOP RIGHT** Fruit and vegetable sellers in the outdoor market in Brastagi, western Sumatra. In the foreground are bunches of *pete,* a tree-grown broad bean in foot-long pods. The beans are popular as a fried snack. **BOTTOM** Neatly arranged fruit baskets in a stall overlooking Lake Batur, Penelokan, Bali.

kare ayam Makassar chicken curry with lemon grass and laos, a specialty of Ujung Pandang, South Sulawesi.

kare telur dengan udang curried eggs and shrimp.

karedok a fresh, raw vegetable salad served with peanut sauce, strongly flavored with *kencur,* or lesser galangal, a pungent rhizome of the ginger family. It is a local treat of Bogor, West Java.   **REGIONAL CLASSIC**

keciput a small cake topped with sesame seeds.

kedoya chicken soup served with giblets and fried eggs.

keik ubi a sweet potato cake with candied lemon peel and raisins.

kelepon (klepon) bite-size balls of green-colored, sticky (glutinous) rice and sago flour filled with a thick syrup of palm sugar and rolled in grated coconut. The entire tidbit should be popped into the mouth at once, or the syrup will squirt out.   **IRRESISTIBLE**

kepala ikan istimewa steamed fish head in curry sauce.

kepiting cingkong goreng tepung crab claws fried in batter made of manioc (cassava) flour.

kerabu a salad of unripe fruit or raw vegetables.

kerak coklat a sweet made with chocolate and chunks of burned rice taken from a pot of rice that has been overheated.

keria a cake made of potatoes, flour and sugar.

kering tempe dried strips of spicy, fried tempe.

ketan bubuk sticky (glutinous) rice flour topped with grated coconut and finely ground peanuts.

ketan dadiah sticky (glutinous) rice mixed with buffalo yogurt.

ketan durian fresh *durian* fruit eaten with sticky (glutinous) rice.

ketan kolak sticky (glutinous) rice with bananas cooked in palm sugar and coconut milk.

ketan serikaya coconut cream custard.   **DELICIOUS**

ketimus a cake made of corn or manioc (cassava) with coconut and palm sugar.

ketiwul steamed manioc (cassava) flour with grated coconut and palm sugar.

ketoprak a salad of bean sprouts, tofu and rice noodles with soy sauce, and sweet and sour peanut sauce. It is a specialty of Jakarta, Java.   **REGIONAL CLASSIC**

ketupat a firm rice cake made by boiling rice in a case woven out of young coconut fronds. The rice expands and becomes compressed within the case. Cooked cakes are removed from the case, sliced into pieces and eaten cold. It is a specialty for   **NATIONAL FAVORITE**

Lebaran, the feast celebrating the end of the month long fast of Puasa (Ramadan). Also called *kupat, tupat* and *nasi ketupat*.

SCRUMPTIOUS **ketupat sayur** a soup-like vegetable curry with a rice cake boiled in a case woven out of young coconut fronds.

kilkil (kikil) a rich stew made with goat and cow's hocks; it is an East Javanese specialty.

kimlo a soup-like dish of vegetables and meat.

klio see *kalio*.

REGIONAL CLASSIC **kohu kohu** a salad of smoked tuna, a specialty of the Maluku (formerly Molucca) Islands.

kol isi berkuah stuffed cabbage leaves in broth.

DELICIOUS **kolak pisang** a sweet compote made with bananas stewed in coconut milk and palm sugar flavored with leaves called *daun pandan*. It is a specialty of Bandar Lampung, South Sumatra.

kolak ubi a sweet compote made with manioc or sweet potatoes stewed in coconut milk and palm sugar.

kroket ayam a chicken croquette.

kuah ikan fish broth.

kuah ketan a sweet sauce for fruit or sweet, sticky (glutinous) rice dishes.

kue batang kayu manis cinnamon-stick cookies.

kue bendera a multi-colored layer cake of rice flour.

kue cubit any of several sweet finger foods sold by street vendors, especially around schools and shops.

TASTY **kue dadar** pink or light-green pancakes rolled around fruit, palm sugar and grated coconut fillings.

kue dokok dokok a cake made of coconut, rice flour, sugar and bananas, which is wrapped in a banana leaf and steamed.

kue kelapa coconut cake.

kue labu pumpkin cake.

kue lidah kucing cat's tongue cookies.

kue madu honey and spice cake.

NATIONAL FAVORITE **kue mangkuk** a colored, rice flour cupcake. The steam released during baking causes the cake's surface to erupt into characteristic points. It is named after the cup, or *mangkuk,* in which it is baked. Another name for this cupcake is *bolu mekar*.

kue pancung individual, crescent-shaped cakes made of rice flour, coconut and sugar.

kue thok a savory treat made with sticky (glutinous) rice flour filled with mung bean paste.

kupat see *ketupat.*

kurma dengan amandel a date and almond confection.

laksa a soup-like dish of rice noodles, chicken, hard-boiled eggs, scallions and bean sprouts in chicken broth and coconut milk, flavored with ginger and turmeric. It typically is served with a side dish of fried shrimp flakes to be added as desired for flavor. — EXCELLENT CHOICE

lalampa a small cake made with sticky (glutinous) rice cooked in coconut milk and filled with a smoked tuna mixture. It is grilled in a banana leaf. This dish is a specialty of Manado, North Sulawesi.

lalap (lalapan) a salad of raw vegetables with spicy sauce; it is a Sundanese (West Javanese) specialty. Each vegetable in the salad is thought to cure a specific ailment such as infertility, high blood pressure or insomnia. — REGIONAL CLASSIC

lapis daging braised meat slices.

lapis legit a multi-layered spice cake; after the first thin layer is baked beneath a grill, it is brushed with melted butter or margarine. Additional thin layers are baked, one at a time, on the previously baked one, until the cake is at least ten layers thick. This cake originates with the Dutch, who call it *spekkoek.*

lapis Malang cakes made with thick, colored layers arranged in horizontal stacks or rolled like jelly-rolls.

lapis Surabaya a three-layer cake made with two vanilla layers separated by a chocolate one. A jam filling separates each layer. — GREAT

lauk a side dish, especially meat or fish served with rice.

lawar a traditional Balinese dish containing grated coconut, spices, fresh blood and any of several combinations of minced meat and finely chopped (slivered) vegetables, leaves and fruits. Blood uniformly coats and reddens the ingredients. The name of each *lawar* indicates its key ingredient. Unless one asks for a *lawar* without blood, *lawar putih,* the dish will contain it. — INTERESTING

lawar daun belimbing *lawar* with leaves from the starfruit plant.

lawar kacang panjang *lawar* with yard-long beans.

lawar nangka *lawar* with jackfruit.

lawar pare *lawar* with bitter melon.

lawar putih see *lawar.*

lawar tulen *lawar* with meat but no vegetables.

lemang the West Sumatran name for white sticky (glutinous) rice cooked with thick coconut milk in green bamboo segments — GREAT lined with young banana leaves. Also called *nasi lemang.* Rice prepared in this manner is called *nasi jaha* by the Minahasans in North Sulawesi and *pa'piong* by the Torajans in South Sulawesi.

lembayung a salad made with the young leaves of the yard-long bean plant.

lemet a cake of grated coconut steamed in banana leaves or corn husks.

NATIONAL FAVORITE **lemper** a sweet snack made of sticky (glutinous) rice with some chicken or a dried meat mixture in the center. It is wrapped in a banana leaf.

lenjeran see *empek empek.*

lidah bakar grilled tongue.

lidah goreng fried tongue.

lompong sagu a sweet made of boiled sago filled with coconut and palm sugar.

lontog Balinese sweet and sticky food made of sticky (glutinous) rice steamed in banana leaves.

NATIONAL FAVORITE **lontong** rice wrapped in a banana leaf and boiled. The rice expands and becomes compressed within the leaf. It is sliced and served cold.

lontong kupang tiny shellfish in broth containing chunks of compressed rice. It is a specialty of Surabaya, East Java.

REGIONAL CLASSIC **lotek** cooked vegetables with peanut sauce flavored with lesser galangal, a pungent rhizome of the ginger family. It is a specialty of Bandung, West Java.

REGIONAL CLASSIC **lumpia** spring roll; it is a specialty of Semarang, Central Java.

lumpia pisang a thin pancake wrapped around a banana.

magadip chicken cooked in spicy broth, a specialty of the island of Madura.

mangut ikan fish in spicy coconut milk, wrapped in a banana leaf.

WONDERFUL **martabak** a savory crepe made with thin dough filled with spicy minced meat, eggs and vegetables. The crepe is then folded into a square and fried. Its thickness depends on the number of eggs ordered.

martabak manis a crepe with a sweet filling. Thin crepes are crispy; thick ones are like pancakes.

masak hijau spicy (hot) chicken with green chili peppers and tomatoes, a specialty of South Kalimantan.

mata sapi dengan sawi fried eggs with shredded Chinese cabbage.

mendut a cake made of sticky (glutinous) rice with grated coconut and palm sugar wrapped in banana leaves.

mi (mie) bakso egg noodle soup with meatballs.   NATIONAL FAVORITE

mi bakso kuah meatballs with noodles in broth.

mi godog see *mi rebu*s.

mi goreng stir-fried egg noodles with bits of vegetables, and   NATIONAL FAVORITE
sometimes meat or shrimp.

mi goreng pakai daging stir-fried egg noodles with meat and bits of vegetables.

mi Jawa rebus Javanese-style noodle soup with cubed beef, cabbage, scallions, bean sprouts and sweet soy sauce.

mi kocok soup with egg noodles, beef knuckle, leeks, chili   REGIONAL CLASSIC
peppers and blanched bean sprouts. It is a specialty of Bandung, West Java.

mi kuah noodles in broth.

mi pangsit noodle soup with wontons.

mi rebus boiled egg noodles; also called *mi godog*.

model soup with fish cakes, tofu and cucumber, a specialty of Palembang, South Sumatra. The fish cakes are made out of the mashed knifefish (*belida*) and sago flour mixure used to make *empek empek*.

nagasari a Javanese cake made of rice and corn flours, coconut   DELICIOUS
milk and bananas, steamed in banana leaves.

nasi antur a mixed plate similar to *nasi campur* but the meat typically is from buffalo; it is a specialty of South Sulawesi.

nasi beriyani rice that is flavored and colored yellow with Indian curry spices; it is a local treat of the Acehnese people of North Sumatra.

nasi Bogana a Central Javanese specialty of turmeric rice with chicken in curry sauce, chicken livers, vegetables and hard-boiled eggs.

nasi bungkus a "take-out" meal of rice with meat, vegetables and a condiment, traditionally wrapped in a banana leaf.

nasi campur a mixed platter consisting of rice, meat and fish,   NATIONAL FAVORITE
vegetables, eggs and sauce topped with some crackers called *krupuk*.

nasi didang steamed rice.

nasi empok a dish of rice mixed with corn flour; it is a specialty   REGIONAL CLASSIC
of Malang, East Java. Also called *nasi jagung*.

nasi golong plain rice balls.

nasi goreng fried rice with bits of vegetables and meats.

nasi goreng istimewa fried rice with bits of vegetables and meats, topped with a fried egg or some other embellishment.

nasi gudeg a dish of rice, chicken simmered in spices and coconut milk, hard-boiled duck eggs and young jack fruit, cooked in an earthen pot and served with some crispy beef skin. The dish, sweetened with palm sugar, is a specialty of Yogyakarta, Central Java.

nasi gurih (kurih) see *nasi uduk.*

nasi jagung see *nasi empok.*

nasi jaha see *lemang.*

nasi jamblang a dish of beef, salted fish, dried cow's lung, vegetables and rice. The rice is wrapped in teak leaves to flavor it. This dish is a specialty of Cirebon, West Java.

nasi kabuli (kebuli) rice and fried lamb or chicken with Indian curry sauce. This dish of Arabic origin is especially popular in South Sulawesi.

nasi Kapau rice served with an assortment of meat and vegetable dishes flavored with tamarind, turmeric and hot chili peppers. It is a specialty of Kapau, a small village near Bukittinggi, West Sumatra.

nasi ketupat see *ketupat*

nasi kuning rice flavored and stained yellow with turmeric. It is a ceremonial dish celebrating happy occasions, such as births and weddings. When the rice is served in a cone shape, it is called *nasi tumpeng*. The cone can be decorated with hard-boiled egg slices, nuts and pieces of vegetables.

nasi kunyit sticky (glutinous) rice flavored and stained yellow with turmeric.

nasi langgi rice with dried beef, an omelette and shrimp sauce. It is a specialty of Cirebon, West Java.

nasi lecek porridge.

nasi lemang see *lemang.*

nasi lengat steamed rice.

nasi lengko rice with goat meat grilled on skewers and served with tempe, tofu, cucumber, bean sprouts and peanut sauce. It is a specialty of Cirebon, West Java.

nasi liwet rice cooked entirely by boiling in water (no steaming step). In the Central Javanese city of Surakarta (Solo), it tradionally is served with chicken, giblets, pear-shaped chayote squash cooked in thick coconut milk, and beef skin crackers.

nasi megono a combination plate of rice with meats and vegetables. It is a specialty of Pekalongan, Central Java.

nasi minyak rice boiled in water to which oil is added.

nasi Padang rice served with mainly hot (spicy) side dishes. **SPICY** Eateries serving this West Sumatran specialty of the Minangkabau people have no menus. Rather, the staff brings to the table individual plates of each dish. You just pay for the dishes you eat, regardless of how much of each is sampled.

nasi pecel a sampler plate with small amounts of rice, fried chicken, **GREAT CHOICE** blanched vegetables, tofu, rice noodles and peanut sauce.

nasi pecel lele the same dish as *nasi pecel* with freshwater catfish substituted for chicken.

nasi pulau rice boiled in broth.

nasi putih plain boiled and steamed white rice.

nasi rames a sampler plate with rice and a combination of several classic side dishes. The selection will vary among restaurants and regions.

nasi rawon rice served in a beef broth prepared with *kluwek,* the **UNUSUAL** nut of the *kepayang* tree used as a spice.

nasi santen see *nasi uduk.*

nasi sayur a vegetarian dish of rice with mixed vegetables.

nasi tambah an extra bowl of plain rice intended for all diners in a group, in addition to the portion served with individual orders.

nasi tim steamed rice cakes served in broth.

nasi tim ayam steamed rice with chicken.

nasi timbel cooked, regular (non-sticky) rice rolled up in a banana leaf.

nasi tumpeng see *nasi kuning.*

nasi uduk rice cooked in coconut milk. In Jakarta it traditionally **FABULOUS** is served with fried foods such as chicken, lamb, offal and tofu. Individual portions of rice are served in banana leaves, topped with crispy, fried shallot slices. The meal also includes *pepes,* steamed or baked food wrapped in banana leaves, including tofu- and anchovy-based mixtures. Rice cooked in coconut milk is also called *nasi gurih* and *nasi santen.*

olibol a filled doughnut. It is of Dutch origin.

oncom fried or steamed cakes of fermented peanut residue, the material that is left after the oil has been extracted.

onde onde fried sticky (glutinous) rice-flour balls filled with sweet mung bean paste and coated with sesame seeds.

DELICIOUS **opor ayam** chicken braised and then simmered in coconut milk containing a somewhat tart, sautéed spice mixture. The sauce is a "white" curry because it has no chili peppers. This dish is a specialty of Java. In the Javanese city of Yogyajakarta, it is a component of the traditional single-dish meal called *gudeg.*

orak arik (arak) stir-fried cabbage and eggs.

orok orok steamed rice flour and palm sugar.

otak goreng deep-fried brains.

REGIONAL CLASSIC **otak otak** a snack of fish steamed in banana leaves. It is a specialty of Sulawesi.

ote ote a fritter of meat or seafood.

pa'piong (pakpiung) see *lemang.*

pacari a curry of pineapple and coconut.

paduan hijau avocado and orange salad.

pais ikan fillet of fish coated with spices and baked in a banana leaf. It is a West Javanese specialty.

panada a pasty filled with smoked tuna. It is a specialty of the Minahasan people of North Sulawesi.

REGIONAL CLASSIC **pangek ayam Padang** a dish of yard-long beans and fried chicken in spicy (hot) coconut milk. Fried chicken is added to the bean mixture after the coconut milk sauce is partially reduced. It is cooked until almost dry. This dish is a specialty of the Minangkabau people of West Sumatra.

GREAT **pangsit** a small dumpling made of a wonton skin filled with meat or seafood, and served in broth.

pangsit goreng a small, deep-fried dumpling made with a wonton skin filled with meat or seafood.

panjang see *empek empek.*

papeda sago porridge.

paruik a West Sumatran sausage filled with a seasoned, beaten duck egg mixture.

pastel a turnover.

pastel Jawa kecil a small shrimp-filled turnover.

pecel a mixed salad of blanched vegetables served with spicy peanut sauce.

EXCELLENT CHOICE **pecel lontong** *pecel* with a side dish of slices of compressed, regular rice cooked in a banana leaf.

peda bakar Pariaman a salted, herring-like fish grilled and served with a spicy (hot) chili pepper sauce. It is a specialty of Pariaman, West Sumatra.

pelecing kankung water spinach in a sauce of hot chili peppers, shrimp paste and lime juice. It is a specialty of Lombok, Nusatenggara.   REGIONAL CLASSIC

pempek (pe empek) see *empek empek*.

pempek kapal selam see *empek empek*.

pempek te!ur see *empek empek*.

pepeda a gooey porridge made from sago. It is a specialty of Ambon, Maluku Islands.

pepes bumbu Bali pieces of fish flavored with a typical Balinese spice mixture of ginger, laos, lesser galangal (see *kencur, Foods & Flavors Guide*), turmeric, dried fish paste, mild chili peppers, garlic and fried shallot flakes in coconut milk, then rolled up and steamed in a banana leaf.   REGIONAL CLASSIC

pepes ikan kembung isi a South Sumatran dish of stuffed fish steamed in banana leaves.

pepes ikan teri a spicy (hot) mixture containing anchovy fry rolled up in a banana leaf and steamed.

pepes oncom a (spicy) hot mixture of fermented peanuts or soybeans rolled in a banana leaf and steamed.   GREAT

perkedel (pergedel) a croquette.

perkedel jagung see *bakwan jagung*.

perkedel kentang a potato croquette.

perkedel kentang dengan daging a potato and meat croquette.

petis a condiment made from jellied shrimp shells or fermented fish, which is used as a seasoning.

pilus boiled balls of grated sweet potato.

pindang bandeng milkfish cooked in water with spices.

pindang iga sapi beef ribs in broth with tamarind and soy sauce.

pindang serani ikan salm whole salmon simmered in broth flavored with shallots, garlic, ginger, laos, turmeric and lemon grass.   DELICIOUS

pindang telur eggs boiled in a guava leaf.

piong duku babi a mixture of minced pork, spices and chopped manioc (cassava) leaves in coconut milk and fresh pork blood, cooked in green bamboo sections. It is a specialty of the Batak people in North Sumatra.   REGIONAL CLASSIC

pisang goreng deep-fried, coated bananas.

podeng roti bread pudding.

puding kelapa muda a firm, sliceable pudding of young coconut meat and raisins. It is a South Sumatran specialty.

pukis Banyumas a molded butter cake, a specialty of the Central Javanese city of Banyumas.

pulu mara boiled fish in savory sauce. It is a specialty of Ujung Pandang, South Sulawesi.

FABULOUS **putu buluh** a treat of rice and palm sugar steamed in a section of bamboo. After the mixture is removed from the bamboo, it is sprinkled with grated coconut and served in a piece of banana leaf.

rakik (rikik) pisang crispy deep-fried banana slices.

rakik (rikik) ubi crispy, deep-fried sweet potato slices.

REGIONAL CLASSIC **rawon** a spicy meat stew flavored and colored black with *kluwek,* the nut of the *kepayang* tree used as a spice. It is a specialty of East Java.

rebus kol boiled cabbage.

rempah deep-fried balls or patties made of ground meat and soft (young) coconut meat.

rempah kelapa deep-fried savory balls of grated coconut.

rempeyek cendawan kecil a fritter made with mushrooms and rice flour.

rempeyek jagung corn fritters.

GREAT CHOICE **rempeyek kacang** thin and crispy savory peanut wafers that look like peanut brittle.

rempeyek kelapa thin and crispy coconut wafers.

rempeyek udang thin and crispy shrimp fritters.

EXTRAORDINARY **rendang** beef simmered in coconut milk and spices, until the water evaporates and the coconut milk turns to oil. The meat absorbs the oil and becomes coated with residue from the oil (*blondo*) and spices. Food cooked this way remains unspoiled for several weeks without refrigeration, and is typical road food for long-distance travelers. It is a specialty of the Minangkabau people of West Sumatra, who sometimes add red beans to the spice paste to enhance the flavor. Other meats and fruits also are cooked this way. Popular versions contain chicken (*rendang ayam*), duck (*rendang itik*) or unripe jackfruit (*rendang nangka*).

rendang ayam see *rendang.*

rendang ikik see *rendang.*

rendang nangka see *rendang.*

rengginang a sticy (glutinous) rice sweetmeat.

romhorn a cone-shaped puff pastry of Dutch origin filled with pastry cream and dusted with sugar.

ronde a warm Javanese drink sold in *warungs* and by street vendors, made of raw peanuts, fruit slices and balls made of sticky (glutinous) rice flour in ginger syrup diluted in hot water.   WONDERFUL

roti bakar bread toasted on a grill.

roti jala a lacy pancake made by drizzling thin streams of batter into a heated frying pan. A special container with small openings at the bottom is used to produce the streams of batter to form the lacy effect. This specialty of North Sumatra is typically eaten with curried lamb or goat.   REGIONAL CLASSIC

rujak a spicy (hot), sweet sauce with shrimp paste, palm sugar, chili peppers and tamarind, used in salads of vegetables or raw, tart (unripe) fruits.   NATIONAL FAVORITE

rujak buah a plate of raw, tart fruit in *rujak*.

rujak cingur a salad of green mango, cucumber, bean sprouts and bull snout in a dark sauce made with fermented shrimp or fish.

rujak penganten a leafy vegetable salad with cucumbers and hard boiled eggs in peanut sauce.

rumbah greens eaten with rice.

sagon a sweet cookie made of rice flour and coconut.

saksang roast pig cooked with pork blood, a specialty of the Batak in North Sumatra, and people in North Sulawesi.   REGIONAL CLASSIC

sambal babi spicy pork relish.

sambal bajak fried chili pepper relish.

sambal bawang spicy onion relish.

sambal buncis spicy green bean relish.

sambal dadak a condiment made to order.

sambal godok a relish of boiled vegetables.

sambal goreng a condiment made by embellishing the basic spicy (hot) red pepper relish (*sambal ulek*) with the addition of chopped red onion, garlic, shrimp paste, laos, lemon juice, chopped tomato and coconut milk.

sambal goreng telur a spicy egg condiment.

sambal goreng tempe matchstick-size pieces of tempe sautéed in a sauce of spices and chili peppers combined with palm sugar, tamarind juice and dried shrimp paste.

sambal goreng tomat spicy tomato relish.

sambal goreng udang asam piquant fried shrimp relish.

sambal goreng udang pete a condiment of chopped beans called *pete* and shrimp, fried in spicy (hot) chili pepper sauce.

sambal hati spicy liver relish.

NATIONAL FAVORITE **sambal kacang** spicy peanut relish; it is the favored condiment for *sate*. The paste is also called *bumbu sate*.

sambal kecap soy sauce and chili pepper condiment.

sambal korek a condiment of tempe.

sambal mantah a Balinese condiment of hot chili peppers, shallots, lemon grass, fish paste and lime.

sambal oncom a relish made with fermented peanut paste, the residue left extracting their oil.

sambal tauco a condiment made with fermented, yellow soybeans.

sambal terasi shrimp paste and chili pepper condiment.

sambal ulek a basic relish of crushed, spicy (hot) red chili peppers with water and salt.

NATIONAL FAVORITE **sate** marinated pieces of meat, seafood or offal threaded on thin bamboo skewers and grilled. Some *sates* are made with ground meat. All are typically served with peanut sauce.

sate ampla chicken gizzards grilled on skewers.

sate asam manis kambing chunks of lamb or goat in sweet-sour sauce grilled on thin bamboo skewers.

sate ayam Pasuruan chicken grilled on skewers and served with peanut sauce. It is a specialty of the city of Pasuruan in East Java.

sate ayam tusuk grilled balls of minced chicken on skewers.

sate babi kecil small cubes of grilled pork served on toothpicks.

sate Bali asam a piquant paste of minced, spiced pork rolled around thick skewers and grilled.

GOOD CHOICE **sate Bali empol** a paste of chopped meat, spices and coconut milk rolled around thick skewers and grilled.

sate Bali kebelet a paste of liver covered by a paste of chopped meat, spices and coconut milk, rolled around thick skewers and grilled.

sate Bali limbat (lembat) a paste of chopped meat, spices and grated coconut rolled around thick skewers and grilled.

EXTRAORDINARY **sate buntel** balls of minced lamb and onion wrapped in caul and grilled on skewers; it is a specialty of Surakarta (Solo), Central Java.

sate empal ikan fish balls grilled on skewers.

sate ikan belida balls of minced knifefish and sago flour steamed in a banana leaf, but not skewered and grilled as the name *sate* would suggest. **TASTY**

sate kalong pieces of beef pounded very flat and grilled on skewers. They are flavored with a sweet spice mixture and served with a special sauce. This specialty of Cirebon, West Java, is sold by vendors who begin selling in the early evening when the fruit bats (*kalong*) also make their appearance. **REGIONAL CLASSIC**

sate kambing skewered and grilled lamb.

sate kelinci rabbit meat grilled on skewers; it is a specialty of Tawangmangu, Central Java. **REGIONAL CLASSIC**

sate kerang clams grilled on bamboo skewers; it is a specialty of Surabaya, East Java.

sate lilit ayam spices and chicken meat pounded to a paste and wrapped around thick skewers and grilled.

sate Manado small pieces of marinated pork grilled on skewers; it is a specialty of Manado, North Sulawesi.

sate manis small pieces of meat marinated in sauce containing palm sugar and sweet soy sauce, then grilled on skewers. **DELICIOUS**

sate Padang pieces of marinated offal grilled on skewers, a specialty of West Sumatra.

sate panas an assortment of foods hot from the grill.

sate pentul balls of minced pork wrapped like drumsticks around skewers and grilled; this Balinese specialty is also called *sate pusut*. **REGIONAL CLASSIC**

sate penyu pieces of turtle meat grilled on skewers. This Balinese specialty is not as prevalent today because turtles are protected.

sate pusut see *sate pentul*.

sate udang shrimp grilled on skewers.

saus Bali a characteristic sauce made of red chili peppers, shallots, garlic, ginger, laos, lesser galangal, turmeric, garlic, fermented shrimp paste, leaves from the Indonesian laurel tree, and coconut milk. It has no sugar, soy sauce or souring agent.

saus kacang peanut sauce.

sawut a snack of grated, steamed manioc (cassava) with palm sugar.

sayur ares a sour soup-like dish of boiled young banana tree stems. **INTERESTING**

sayur asam a sour soup-like dish of mixed vegetables with the young nuts and leaves of the *melinjo* tree, flavored with tamarind and fermented fish paste. **GREAT**

sayur asam ikan a spicy (hot) and sour soup-like dish of fish.

sayur bayam a soup-like dish of spinach in coconut milk.

GREAT **sayur brongkos** a dish of mixed vegetables in sour sauce containing coconut milk, flavored and blackened with *kluwek* nuts, the fruit of the *kepayang* tree.

sayur daun belimbing a soup-like dish of starfruit leaves in coconut milk.

sayur gudeg a soup-like dish of unripe jackfruit cooked in coconut milk and spices.

sayur ikan baung a hot and sour soup-like vegetable dish with freshwater catfish called *baung*.

sayur kare a soup-like dish of curried vegetables.

REGIONAL CLASSIC **sayur lodeh** mixed vegetables blanched in coconut milk and flavored with the leaves and nuts (outer skin) of the *melinjo* tree. It is a specialty of Cirebon, West Java.

sayur nangka dan ares a Balinese soup-like dish of unripe jackfruit and boiled, young banana tree stems in coconut milk.

sayur tumis stir-fried vegetables.

sayur urap see *urap*.

sekoteng a ginger-flavored drink with peanuts, served hot.

EXCELLENT **semanggi** chunks of potatoes, boiled bean sprouts and the steamed leaves of a small aquatic variety of clover, topped with a spicy sauce of mashed sweet potatoes and fermented fish or shrimp paste. This specialty of Surabaya, East Java, is served in a banana leaf and eaten with rice crackers.

semar mendem meat-filled sticky (glutinous) rice cakes wrapped in an egg pancake rather than a banana leaf.

semur daging slices of beef cooked in spices and soy sauce.

semur hati braised liver in soy sauce and spices.

REGIONAL CLASSIC **sepat ayam** shredded chicken in a coconut-based sour sauce with unripe mango, a specialty of Sumbawa, Nusatenggara.

serabi a pancake made with rice flour and coconut milk; it is a specialty of Cirebon, West Java.

SCRUMPTIOUS **serikaya (srikaya)** coconut cream custard, flavored with aromatic leaves called *daun pandan*. (see *Foods & Flavors Guide*).

serombotan a Balinese salad of both raw and cooked vegetables topped with spicy grated coconut.

serundeng a garnish of roasted shredded coconut.

serundeng kacang a garnish of fried peanuts.

singgang ayam spread-eagled chicken cooked in coconut milk and spices, and then roasted until the skin is crispy. It is a specialty of the Minangkabau people of West Sumatra, and is often the featured dish at weddings.

slada buncis dengan tauge a salad of green beans and bean sprouts.

slada mentimun cucumber salad.

sop buntut oxtail soup. *EXCELLENT*

sop buntut Gladag oxtail soup with carrots, leeks and potatoes. It is a specialty of Gladag, a village close to Surakarta (Solo), Central Java.

sop kaki sapi a soup with buffalo hocks.

sop kambing a soup of lamb or goat head, hocks and tripe. This *sop* is unusual because the broth includes cow's milk.

sop kambing jeroan a soup of goat or lamb giblets.

sop sayuran a soup-like dish with mixed vegetables in coconut-based broth.

soto ayam chicken soup.

soto ayam Lamongan chicken soup made with shrimp stock and topped with fried garlic or chopped cashews. It is a specialty of Lamongan, East Java. *REGIONAL CLASSIC*

soto babat tripe soup.

soto babat telur tripe soup with hard-boiled eggs.

soto Bandung beef soup with fried soybeans, daikon radish and lemon grass in clear broth. It is a specialty of the West Javanese city of Bandung. *EXTRAORDINARY*

soto Banjar chicken broth, sometimes mixed with milk, with cellophane noodles, hard-boiled duck eggs, and chunks of compressed rice steamed in small cases woven of coconut palm fronds. Potato fritters are served with the soup. It is a specialty of the Banjar people of South Kalimantan. *REGIONAL CLASSIC*

soto Betawi beef soup with meat, tripe, offal and potatoes. It is a dish originating with the Betawi ethnic group indigenous to the Javanese city of Jakarta.

soto koyah lamb or chicken soup with ground peanuts and powdered coconut. It is a specialty of the East Javanese city of Malang.

soto kudus komplit chicken soup with bean sprouts and quail eggs.

soto Madura beef soup with meat, tripe and tail. It is a specialty of the island of Madura.

soto Makassar campur see *coto* Makassar *campur*.

soto Medan chicken or beef soup in a coconut-based broth, served with a potato croquette. It is a specialty of Medan, North Sumatra. *FABULOUS*

REGIONAL CLASSIC **soto mi (mie)** beef soup with noodles, tomatoes and cabbage. It is a specialty of Jakarta, Java.

soto Pekalongan beef and vegetable soup with tripe and fermented soybean paste. It is a specialty of the Central Javanese city of Pekalongan.

soto sumsum (sungsum) marrow soup.

soto Tegal beef soup with vegetables, tripe and cellophane noodles; it is a specialty of the Central Javanese city of Tegal.

spekkoek see *lapis legit.*

sup kol kembang cauliflower soup.

REGIONAL CLASSIC **susu segar madu telur** a mixture of fresh milk, honey and beaten eggs, considered a macho, invigorating drink to increase virility and health. This specialty of Surakarta (Solo), Central Java, is often abbreviated SMT on menus—or even on buildings!

tahu bacem tofu steeped in a mixture of palm sugar, coriander and garlic in water, boiled until dry, then fried. It is a Central Javanese dish.

REGIONAL CLASSIC **tahu campur Lamongan** a stew of sliced beef brisket, tofu, noodles, bean sprouts and hot chili peppers, served with fried manioc (cassava) and shredded lettuce. It is a specialty of the East Javanese city of Lamongan.

tahu goreng fried tofu.

tahu goreng kecap fried tofu with soy sauce.

tahu telur tofu omelette.

tai kuda see *buah jingah.*

talam a rice-flour cake filled with shredded chicken or palm sugar.

DELICIOUS **tape (tapai)** a mildly alcoholic snack made from boiled or steamed black, sticky (glutinous) rice. It is usually served with *lemang,* white sticky rice cooked in a bamboo container lined with young banana leaves in thick coconut cream. This snack is especially popular during the Muslim month of fasting and in the feast (Lebaran) that celebrates its end.

tauco ikan fish in yellow bean sauce with stir-fried vegetables.

tauge goreng fried bean sprouts with noodles, *oncom* and chives. It is a specialty of Bogor, West Java.

teh poci Tegal rock sugar and jasmine tea made in a clay pot; it is a specialty of the Central Javanese city of Tegal.

teh talua Pariaman Pariaman-style tea, which contains an egg yolk. The city of Pariaman is in West Sumatra.

tekwan a soup with fish balls made of sago flour mixed with minced knifefish flesh. It is a specialty of Palembang, South Sumatra.   REGIONAL CLASSIC

telur bumbu Bali hard-boiled eggs in a sauce containing the typical Balinese mixture of spices (see *bumbu* Bali, *Foods & Flavors Guide*).

telur dadar pedas hot chili peppers rolled in an egg pancake.

telur pindang eggs marbled by soaking in soy sauce or in a solution of steeped guava leaves, shallot skins, laos and turmeric leaf.

telur rebus hard-boiled eggs.

tempe goreng thin strips of tempe fried with palm sugar and chili peppers.

tempe mendoan a thin, fermented soybean cake individually wrapped in a banana leaf. Cakes are made by firmly compressing the soybean mixture until it is no more than the width of a single layer of beans. They are lightly deep-fried in rice flour batter and served with rice and leeks and a condiment of green chili peppers. This preparation is a specialty of Banyumas, Central Java.   REGIONAL CLASSIC

terik spicy tempe.

tetel sticky (glutinous) rice steamed in coconut milk, mashed and mixed with grated coconut.

timlo Solo clear chicken soup with rice; it is a special preparation of Surakarta (Solo), Central Java.

tinombur a spice paste containing *andaliman,* or jungle pepper. It is a favorite of the Batak people of North Sumatra.   UNUSUAL

tinutuan see *bubur* Manado.

tiwul savory or sweet snacks made of manioc (cassava) flour.

tongseng kambing lamb sautéed in a hot (spicy) sauce and cooked with cabbage.

tum a Balinese dish of ground duck or chicken mixed with spices and steamed in a banana leaf.

tum hati ayam a Balinese dish of minced chicken livers mixed with spices and grated coconut, and steamed in a banana leaf.   EXCELLENT

tum pepe a Balinese dish of mushrooms with leaves called *pepe,* mixed together in a sauce and steamed in a banana leaf.

tumis bajam stir-fried spinach.

tumis kacang kapri stir-fried pea pods.

tumis tauge stir-fried bean sprouts.

tumpeng a ceremonial dish of plain cooked rice, often stained yellow with turmeric, served in a cone shape. Also called *tumpeng selamatan* and *nasi tumpeng.*

tupat see *ketupat.*

udang goreng tepung batter-fried shrimp.

udang rebus boiled shrimp.

uli a mixture of sticky (glutinous) rice cooked with coconut, which resembles polenta. It is sliced and served with *tetel.*

EXCELLENT   **urap (urab)** blanched vegetables tossed with a mixture of spices and grated coconut. Also called *sayur urap.*

wajik a square-shaped dessert of sticky (glutinous) rice and palm sugar.

warembol a light bread bun.

wedang kacang putih see *bubur kacang tanah.*

DELICIOUS   **wedang ronda** a soupy, ginger water dessert with unroasted peanuts, colored balls of sticky (glutinous) rice flour filled with chopped peanuts, and *kolang kaling,* the fruits of the *aren* palm. It is a specialty of West Java.

TASTY   **wiengko Babat** giant, glutinous, coconut pancakes, which are a specialty of the town of Babat near Surabaya, East Java.

Foods & Flavors Guide

This chapter is a comprehensive list of foods, spices, kitchen utensils and cooking terminology in Indonesian, with English translations. The list will be helpful in interpreting menus since it is impossible to cover all the flavors or combinations possible for certain dishes. It will also be useful for shopping in both supermarkets and the lively and fascinating outdoor markets.

abon meat that has been boiled, shredded and then fried. Often spicy, it can be a topping on dishes such as *nasi rames* or *nasi rawon* (see *Menu Guide*).

acar pickles; also a common condiment containing cucumbers and other vegetables (see *Menu Guide*).

aceh see *rambutan*.

adas dill; it is also the name for the seeds and leaves of fennel. Another word for fennel is *adas pedas*.

adas manis aniseed; also called *anis* and *jintan manis*.

adas pedas see *adas*.

agar agar a thickening agent obtained from seaweed, which produces a gelatin-like consistency without chilling. It is sold in the markets in sheets or in powdered form.

air water.

air jeruk orange juice.

air kapur limewater. It is used in certain desserts made of sticky (glutinous) rice flour that require a firm texture. Also used in making candied fruit to prevent the fruits from becoming mushy in boiling sugar syrup.

air kelapa coconut water.

air minum drinking water.

air putih "white," or purified, water; it is typically achieved by boiling.

Ajinomoto monosodium glutamate (MSG); it is actually a brand name.

aliah see *jahe*.

alpokat (advokat) avocado; also spelled *pokat*. Another word for avocado is *buah mentega*.

ambetan see *durian*.

ambu ambu bonito.

FOODS & FLAVORS GUIDE

amandel almond.

ampela chicken gizzard; also called *rempela*.

ampiang cooked, dried and flattened grains of plain or sticky rice.

anak itik duckling.

andaliman jungle pepper. The small, dark green berries have a lemony taste and impart a slight numbing sensation to the mouth. It is a key ingredient in the North Sumatran condiment called *tinombur*, which is served with grilled or roasted goldfish (see *Menu Guide*). Also called *intir intir*.

aneka assorted.

anggur grape.

anggur kering dried currant or raisin; another name for raisin is *kismis*.

angsa goose; also spelled *gangsa*.

angsio food braised in a dark liquid such as soy sauce.

anis see *adas manis*.

antah see *kulit padi*.

apel apple.

aprikot apricot.

arak a strong, brandy-like alcoholic beverage made by distilling any of several beer-like drinks (*tuak*), which are made from fermented sticky (glutinous) rice or from the juice (sap) of unopened flowers from various types of palm trees, especially the coconut palm (see *tuak,* this *Guide*).

arbei strawberry.

aren the sugar palm. Its juice (sap) is boiled down to make brown sugar (*gula merah*) or is fermented to make a yeasty, beer-like drink (*tuak*). The sugar palm fruits (*kolang kaling*) are enjoyed in drinks and desserts (see individual entries, this *Guide*).

ares the stem of a young banana plant, which is chopped up, cooked and eaten as a vegetable.

arnab rabbit. Also called *kelinci* and *terwelu*.

arvi yam.

asam (asem) sour. *Asam* is also the name for the tamarind, a fruit with sour, sticky, red-brown pulp. Both fresh fruit and blocks of hard, preserved pulp are available in the markets. Another name for tamarind is *asam Jawa*.

asam glugur a very tart fruit whose flesh and skin are used as a souring agent.

asam Jawa see *asam*.

asam kandis a small, sweet fruit with thin, bitter skin that is dried for use as a souring agent. When dried, the skin is hard and black. Except for the dissimilar coloration, pieces of it resemble stale dried apricots.

asam kincung a pineapple-like fruit used to impart tartness to certain dishes such as *gulai ikan kakap* (see *Menu Guide*).

asam manis sweet and sour foods; the flavor is attributable to a combination of vinegar and sugar.

asam pedas hot (spicy)-sour food. It is a characteristic West Sumatran (Minangkabau) flavor combination used in cooking fresh meat or dried fish. The meat or fish, especially anchovy, is cooked in hot and sour chili sauce without coconut milk.

asin salty.

asinan salted or pickled foods.

asli genuine.

ati see *hati*.

ayam chicken.

ayam belanda turkey; also called *ayam kalkun*.

ayam kampung a free-running chicken.

ayam kalcun see *ayam belanda*.

babat tripe (cow).

babi pig; can also mean pork. Indonesia's population is mainly Muslim, limiting the availability of pork to non-Muslim parts of the Indonesian archipelago or to Chinese-run restaurants and markets.

babi asap smoked pork, bacon or ham.

bacem marinated.

badam almond.

badam hijau pistachio.

badeg (badek) an alcoholic beverage made from fermented cassava or rice.

bagar see *kare*.

bahan pangan foodstuff.

bakar barbecued or grilled.

bakasang a North Sulawesi seasoning similar to shrimp paste, or *trasi,* which is made from fermented sardine or bonito intestines.

bakmi (bakmie) egg noodles, either fried (*bakmi goreng*) or in soup (see *Menu Guide*). This word is of Chinese origin and initially meant pork with noodles but has become a generic word for egg noodles. *Mi* (*mie*) also means egg noodles.

bakso meatballs; also a soup (see *Menu Guide*); can be spelled *baso* or *ba'so*.

bakwan deep-fried fritters.

balado a dish cooked in red chili pepper sauce, as opposed to being accompanied by a condiment, or *sambal,* of red chili pepper sauce.

bale see *ikan*.

balok palm wine.

balur jerky or dried meat.

bandang large; other words for large are *besar* and *gede*.

bandeng the milkfish. It is a popular freshwater fish despite its many bones. In the markets, it is available fresh, salted and smoked.

bangkuang jicama.

barak red, sticky (glutinous) rice. It is not highly regarded.

baronang a large, popular fish with very few bones, which is typically grilled.

baso (ba'so) see *bakso*.

batu giling the slightly curved, granite stone (mortar) and smaller, round stone (pestle) used to crush fresh spices and roots such as chili peppers, onions, garlic, ginger and turmeric into a paste.

baung a freshwater catfish.

bawal the pomfret fish. *Bawal hitam* is the black pomfret; *bawal putih* is the white pomfret.

bawang bakung see *bawang kucai*.

bawang Bombay the yellow bulb onion commonly used in the United States.

bawang daun scallion; also called *bawang hijau* or *daun bawang*.

bawang goreng finely sliced shallots, fried and used to garnish many dishes.

bawang hijau see *bawang daun*.

bawang kucai chives; also called *bawang bakung*.

bawang merah shallot; also called *brambang*.

bawang prai leek.

bawang putih garlic; also called *dasun* and *kesune*.

bayam amaranth; it is used as a spinach substitute.

bebanten tall, ornate food offerings borne to the temples on the heads of women. They consist of fruits and small, colorful cupcakes and rice balls artistically arranged in rows, along with fresh flowers, decorations woven from palm leaves and an occasional whole roasted duck, all skewered into a central supporting banana plant stem.

bebek duck; also called *itik*.

bebotok steamed.

bedukang a freshwater catfish.

bekatul see *kulit padi*.

bekil snapper.

belanak gray mullet.

belimbing the carambola, or starfruit, so named because crosswise slices are star-shaped. This oblong, orange-yellow fruit grows to 6 inches in length and has 5 or 6 longitudinal ridges. Its crispy yellow flesh is sour. Also called *belimbing manis*, or sweet starfruit.

belimbing manis see *belimbing*.

belimbing wuluh a small green fruit about 3 inches long, related to the star-fruit. It is used as a souring agent or is candied by boiling in sugar syrup.

beluluk a young, green coconut.

belut eel; also called *mua, pucok nipah* and *remang.*

beras hulled, uncooked rice, as opposed to harvested, unprocessed rice (*padi*) and hulled, cooked rice (*nasi*).

beras beras drumfish.

beras ketan see *ketan.*

beras kuning uncooked rice, colored yellow with turmeric root, used for ceremonial offerings.

beras pulut see *ketan.*

berkil perch.

bertih roasted rice kernels.

besar see *bandang.*

besengek see *bumbu besengek.*

beskit (biskuit) cookie.

betok a type of perch.

bewa an oblong yellow-orange fruit about the size of a large olive.

biasi usual, or regular, as opposed to *komplit,* or "with all the trimmings."

bihun thin rice noodles; also spelled *mihun.*

biji seed or kernel.

binatang buruan dan unggas game and poultry. On menus, these words head the game and poultry section.

bir beer. Indonesian brands are *Anker* and *Bintang.*

bir hitam stout.

bir tongan draft beer.

biri biri see *kambing.*

biu the common name for banana in Bali; elsewhere in Indonesia it is *pisang.* When the varietal name is the same, e.g., *pisang mas* and *biu mas,* this *Guide* will have a single entry, under *pisang.*

biu dang saba a small banana that is black when ripe.

biu gading see *pisang hijau.*

biu gedang saba a papaya-shaped banana.

biu udang the red-skinned shrimp banana.

blego a large green or yellow gourd with white flesh and many seeds at the center. This seeded flesh is discarded and the remainder is chopped into cubes and cooked like pumpkin.

blewa a melon with pumpkin-like grooves and usually splotchy skin, varying in color from green to yellowish-orange.

blondo the sediment left after boiling coconut milk so long that the water has evaporated and coconut oil is left.

blumkol cauliflower; also called *bungkul, kol kembang* and *kubis bunga.*

bolu spongecake.

bon the bill.

bongkrek the residue left after extracting the oil from coconut meat.

bontotan food that travels well, such as rice steamed in banana leaves. Also called *mem bontot.*

brambang see *bawang merah.*

bregedel see *perkedel.*

brem a sweet Balinese wine made from a mixture of fermented black and white sticky (glutinous) rice. The black rice is included for darker color.

buah the generic word for fruit. Note that fruits are named two ways—the specific name alone, or in combination with the generic word *buah.* For example, the word for plum is *prem.* It is written as *prem* or *buah prem.* Although both names are commonly seen, only the specific name, *prem,* will be listed in this *Guide.* Some fruits are always named with both the generic and specific terms. Because of these variations in naming fruit, be sure to look under the specific name and the entries under *buah.* Note also that some vegetables include the initial word *buah* in their name.

buah ara fig.

buah buahan dan kacang kacangan fruits and nuts/legumes. On menus, this phrase heads the fruits and nuts/legumes section.

buah buahan kering dried fruit.

buah buni see *cerme.*

buah campur mixed fruit.

buah ketimun muda a gherkin, the immature fruit of a variety of cucumbers used in pickling.

buah mentega see *alpokat.*

buah nona the sweetsop or sugar apple. It is a round to ovoid green fruit up to 4 inches long with many small bumps studding its surface. The segmented, white pulp is sweet and delicious, tasting somewhat like a pear. Avoid the toxic seeds.

buah per pear.

buah punti a large, sweet banana.

bubuk merica ground pepper.

bubuk roti breadcrumbs; also called *remah roti.*

bubur porridge.

buka open. "*Buka*" signs will be posted at shops and restaurants to indicate they are open for business. Also refers to the meal eaten immediately after sunset during Puasa (Ramadan), the Muslim fasting month.

bulu (buluh) bamboo. In Sumatra, North Sulawesi and West Kalimantan, many food preparations are slow-cooked in freshly cut green bamboo sections. Bamboo is used for steaming sweets made of sticky (glutinous) rice, palm sugar and coconut (*kutu buluh*) and for the production of a rich yogurt made from buffalo milk (*dadiah*), whose curdling is the result of a naturally occurring culture within the bamboo (see *Menu Guide*).

buluan see *rambutan*.

bumbu the general term for a paste of spices.

bumbu Bali a common Balinese spice paste consisting of shallots, fish paste, candlenuts, garlic, fresh laos, fresh turmeric, coriander and hot chili peppers, which is mixed with bruised stalks of lemon grass and added to coconut milk.

bumbu besengek a special spice paste consisting of shallots, garlic, candlenuts, hot red chili peppers, coriander, turmeric, laos, shrimp paste, and lemon grass in coconut milk. Also simply called *besengek*.

bumbu cengkeh pimento.

bumbu tauco a sauce made with fermented soybeans.

buncis green string beans.

bunga lawang star anise.

bunga pala mace. It is the lacy covering, or aril, surrounding the nutmeg seed, which is ground and used as a spice. Also called *fuli* and *sekar pala*.

bungkul see *blumkol*.

bungkus "take-out" food.

buntut tail.

burung dara pigeon.

burung puyuh see *puyuh*.

cabe (cabai) a chili pepper; also called *lombok* and *tabia*.

cabe hijau a green chili pepper; it is milder than the bird's eye chili pepper, or *cabe rawit*.

cabe Jawa a long, fairly mild chili pepper.

cabe merah a red chili pepper; it is milder than the bird's eye chili pepper, or *cabe rawit*.

cabe rawit the bird's eye pepper. It is a tiny, very hot red or green chili pepper, usually crushed with other fresh spices to make a paste or sauce.

caisim Chinese cabbage.

cakalang tuna or skipjack; also called *tongkol*.

cakalang fufu smoked tuna, a North Sulawesi staple.

cakwe a long fritter of twisted dough, which becomes light and airy when fried. It is thinly sliced and sprinkled on top of breakfast rice porridges.

campur mixed.

canggai Shanghai fried, coated peanuts; also called *kacang* Shanghai.

cangkir a cup or small mug.

cangkuk preserved or pickled fish.

cempedak a type of fruit similar to, but smaller than, the jackfruit (*nangka*), which has a strong flavor. It is generally cooked before being eaten.

cencaru the horse mackerel.

cendawan a mushroom; also called *jamur* and *kulat*.

cendol (cindol) small pieces of green-colored rice flour dough added to cold drinks; also the name of a drink, *es cendol* (see *Menu Guide*).

ceng molasses or syrup; also called *gula kinca, gula tetes* and *tengguli*.

cengkaruk fried sticky (glutinous) rice used in making sweetmeats.

cengkeh cloves.

centong a rice ladle.

ceri cherry.

cerme the Otaheite (Tahiti) gooseberry. It is a small, green fruit eaten unripe in a fruit snack called *rujak* or used in cooking as a souring agent (see *Menu Guide*). Also called *buah buni*.

ceroring see *duku*.

ciku see *sawo manila*.

cimplung food candied by boiling with sap or juice that is being boiled down for sugar.

cincang chop or mince.

cingur the cartilage and meat of bull snout and ears; it can be a salad ingredient.

cobek a clay mortar used to grind or crush fresh spices such as ginger, turmeric and chili peppers into a paste. The clay pestle is called *ulek ulek* and *pergulakan* (see this *Guide*).

coklat chocolate.

coklat susu milk chocolate.

contong a cone-shaped food container made out of paper or banana leaves.

copra coconut meat dried to retard spoiling. It is the raw material used to make coconut oil commercially. At home, coconut oil is made from fresh coconut meat broken into chunks or grated, and boiled until the oil rises to the surface and can be removed easily.

coto see *soto*.

cuka vinegar.

cukit fork.

cumi cumi squid; also called *sotong*.

cuncung a cone-shaped pastry with a sweet filling.

dabu dabu a sauce made in North Sulawesi with chopped chili peppers, shallots, tomato, *bakasang*, a paste made of fermented sardine or tuna intestines, and the juice of *lemon cui,* a citrus fruit grown in this area.

dada breast meat.

dadar omelette.

dadiah buffalo yogurt.

daftar makanan the menu.

daftar minuman anggur the wine list.

daging the flesh or meat of the animal as opposed to the innards (*jeroan*). On menus, this word heads the meat section.

daging asap smoked meat.

daging awet preserved meat.

daging babi pork.

daging cacah minced meat; also called *daging cincang*.

daging kambing goat or lamb meat. Since goats are much more common than sheep, a dish with *daging kambing* probably contains goat meat.

daging kerbau water buffalo meat.

daging pinggang meat from the loin.

daging sapi beef.

daing dried meat or fish.

dandang a large metal pot for steaming rice.

dapur kitchen.

dasun see *bawang putih*.

daun the generic word for leaf. Note that leaves are named two ways—the specific name alone, or in combination with the generic word, *daun*. For example, the specific name for basil is *kemangi*. It is written as *kemangi* or *daun kemangi*. Although both names are commonly seen, only the specific name will be listed in this *Guide*. Some leaves are always referred to using both the generic and specific terms. Because of these variations in naming leaves, be sure to look under both the specific name and the entries under *daun*.

daun bawang see *bawang daun*.

daun belimbing the bitter leaves from the starfruit plant, which are used as a vegetable in certain dishes such as *lawar* (see *Menu Guide*).

daun cincau leaves used to make a green gelatin for cold drinks.

daun jeruk purut Kaffir lime leaf. It is the leaf from an Indonesian citrus tree, used dried as a seasoning. See *jeruk purut* (this *Guide*) for a description of the fruit of this tree, the Kaffir lime.

daun jipang leaves from a squash plant (*labu siam*), used as a vegetable.

daun katuk a spinach-like vegetable.

daun ketumbar cilantro.

daun mangkuk the aromatic, cup-shaped leaf from a shrub, which is both a vegetable and a food container. It is a traditional ingredient in the Sumatran dish called *gulai otak,* or brains in spicy coconut sauce (see *Menu Guide*). Also called *godong mangkokan.*

daun melinjo leaves from the *melinjo* tree, which are eaten as a vegetable. The leaves and olive-shaped nuts (*melinjo*) of the tree are traditional components of the dish called *sayur asam* (see *Menu Guide*).

daun pandan fragrant, long, flat leaves of the screwpine, used as a flavoring.

daun papaya leaves of the papaya tree, used as a vegetable.

daun salam aromatic leaves from an Indonesian laurel tree, used whole in many dishes as we use bay leaves. Also called *manting.*

daun sop soup stock vegetables—scallions or leeks, and young celery leaves—banded together, a few pieces each, and sold by the bundle, especially in the markets of North and West Sumatra.

daun suji leaves used to color food light green.

delima pomegranate.

dendang clam.

dendeng a kind of jerky made with thinly sliced meat, usually beef, coated with a spice mixture, cooked and then sun-dried.

dideh see *marus.*

dingin cold.

dorang see *kakap.*

duku the langsat, a small, slightly sour yellow fruit mottled with brown spots. The segmented flesh is translucent white, resembling that of the lychee. Also called *ceroring.*

durian (duren) an ovoid fruit, 6 to 12 inches long, with a thick yellow-green rind, covered with sharp and woody pyramidal spines. The pale yellow pulp resembles custard and, to many, it has a very unpleasant odor. It is eaten fresh and used to flavor ice cream and other desserts. The seeds are eaten, fried or roasted. Another name for this fruit is *ambetan.*

durian belanda see *sirsak.*

ebi small, dried shrimp.

embacang a type of mango with a pungent taste; when overripe, it tastes fermented. Also called *mangga kuini.*

emping fried chips made from pounded and dried *melinjo* nut kernels. They are enjoyed with meals or eaten as a snack. Also see *krupuk.*

encer thin or watery.

ercis see *kacang belimbing.*

es ice; could also be a type of Popsicle.

es krim ice cream.

frambos raspberry.

frikadel see *perkedel*.

fuli see *bunga pala*.

gabus freshwater snakehead fish.

gajebo beef brisket.

gajus see *kacang mete*.

gamat sea cucumber or sea slug; also called *tripang*.

gambas a green squash with longitudinal ridges, which is edible when young. The internal fibrous structure hardens with age, and is used as a bath sponge (loofah). Also called *ketola, oyong* and *petola*.

gandaria a small, sour, orange-colored fruit made into pickles, used in condiments and in the dish called *lalapan* (see *Menu Guide*).

gangsa see *angsa*.

garam salt.

garpu fork.

gayam a pulpy, bland fruit known as the Otaheite (Tahiti) chestnut, eaten cooked. It is sold in the markets already cooked, and is kept in water to retain moisture.

gede see *bandang*.

gelang purslane; also called *krokot*.

genjer an asparagus-tasting aquatic plant cooked and eaten as a vegetable.

gimbal a type of fritter.

ginjal kidney.

glodok mud skipper fish.

godog (godok) boiled; another name for boiled is *rebus*.

godong mangkokan see *daun mangkuk*.

gogo rancah an esteemed variety of non-irrigated (dry) rice.

goreng fried.

gori unripe jackfruit (*nangka*).

gowok a deep purple, cherry-like fruit with sour white flesh and a single, inedible seed. Also known as *kaliasem*.

gula sugar.

gula aren see *gula merah*.

gula gula sweets or candy.

gula hitam caramel.

gula Jawa see *gula merah*.

gula kacang peanut brittle; also called *rempeyek kacang*.

gula kinca see *ceng*.

gula merah palm sugar made from the juice (sap) of certain palm trees, especially the coconut and sugar palms. It is available in the markets in cylindrical blocks or in the shape of the small bowls in which it hardened. Also called *gula* Jawa. Palm sugar made specifically from the *aren* palm is called *gula aren*.

gula pasir granulated cane sugar; also called *gula putih*.

gula putih see *gula pasir*.

gula tetes see *ceng*.

gulai Sumatran-style curried meat, fish or vegetable stew containing lots of sauce. There are many regional variations, with coconut milk a key ingredient in most of them. Some are made tart with the addition of sour fruits such as tamarind, *asam kandis* or *asam glugur*; others are sweetened with palm sugar. These curries generally bear little resemblance to the flavors imparted by curry mixtures associated with Indian cooking. Ginger (and related rhizomes) and chili peppers often provide the main essence of these dishes. *Gule* is the Javanese word for this type of dish.

gule see *gulai*.

guling roulade of meat; it is meat pounded flat and rolled around a filling.

gurami a large and bony native freshwater carp; also called *kalui*.

gurita octopus.

halal an animal slaughtered according to Islamic law by cutting its throat while saying the name of Allah.

has dalam a filet or tenderloin.

hati liver; also spelled *ati*.

hidangan telur see *masakan telur*.

hijau (ijo) green.

hoen kwe (hunkwe) see *tepung kacang hijau*.

Idul Adha the Muslim feast of sacrifice.

Idul Fitri see Lebaran.

iga rib.

ikan the generic name for fish. Note fish are named two ways—the specific name alone, or in combination with the generic word, *ikan*. For example, the specific name for knifefish is *belida*. It is written as *belida* or *ikan belida*. Although both names are commonly seen, only the specific name will be listed in this *Guide*. Some fish always are referred to using both the generic and specific terms. Because of these variations in naming fish, be sure to look under both the specific name and the entries under *ikan*. Another name for fish is *bale*.

ikan asin salted fish.

ikan belida knifefish, a flat, eel-like fish.

ikan bilis small, smoked fish sold in West Sumatra markets.

ikan cucut dogfish, or small shark.

ikan dan makanan hasil laut fish and seafood. On menus, these words head the fish and seafood section.

ikan kembung see *sarden*.

ikan kering dried and salted fish.

ikan lidah sole.

ikan mas freshwater goldfish, or golden carp.

ikan merah red snapper; also called *jenaha* and *kakap merah*.

ikan mujair a small, black, freshwater fish, full of tiny bones.

ikan pedangto swordfish.

ikan saluangan a small, freshwater fish prized in Banjarmasin, South Kalimantan.

ikan sebelah flounder.

ikan teri whitebait.

ikan teri kering dried whitebait, especially anchovy fry.

indring see *selasih*.

injin see *ketan hitam*.

intir intir see *andaliman*.

isi stuffed or filled.

isi perut intestines and bowel. Another word for intestines is *usus*.

istimewa special. If a menu item has this word in its name, expect a fried egg on top, or some other embellishment.

itik see *bebek*.

jagung jali barley.

jagung manis sweet corn, corn on the cob; also called *jagung muda*.

jagung muda see *jagung manis*.

jagung muda kecil small, immature sweet corn on the cob.

jahan catfish.

jahe ginger. It commonly is used fresh, pounded together with other ingredients to make a spice paste. Also called *aliah*.

jajan a sweet or snack bought from vendors or shops; also the name of a fruit-filled pancake (see *Menu Guide*).

jajan pasar assorted traditional cakes.

jambe see *pinang*.

jamblang the Javanese plum. It is an olive-shaped, dark purple fruit with translucent purplish pulp surrounding a large red seed. Also called *juwet*.

jambu the common name for several different types of fruit (see individual entries under *jambu*, this *Guide*).

jambu air the water apple, small, bell-shaped fruits varying in color from white, to several shades of pink, to green. The flesh, almost tasteless, is somewhat spongy. Also called *jambu bol, jambu semarang* and *nyambu*.

jambu air mawar the rose apple; a small, bell-shaped fruit with a rose scent.

jambu batu see *jambu klutuk*.

jambu biji see *jambu klutuk*.

jambu bol see *jambu air*.

jambu klutuk guava; an ovoid, green-skinned fruit with a prominent nipple at one end. The whitish pulp contains many small seeds. Also called *jambu batu* and *jambu biji*.

jambu mete the cashew apple. This bell pepper-shaped yellow or bright-red fruit is about 3 inches long. It is actually a "pseudo fruit" formed from the swollen flower stem. The true fruit is the kidney-shaped cashew nut growing at the tip of the cashew apple (see *kacang mete*, this *Guide*). The yellow pulp, eaten fresh, is very juicy and somewhat acidic. Note that the juice stains clothing indelibly. Also called *nyambu mete*.

jambu semarang see *jambu air*.

jamu herbal medicines or tonics.

jamur see *cendawan*.

jamur tiram oyster or straw mushrooms; also called *shimeji*.

jantung pisang the heart-shaped banana blossom, which is cooked and eaten as a vegetable.

jawawut millet.

jemuju see *jintan*.

jenaha see *ikan merah*.

jengkol a round, somewhat flattened, mildly toxic, light-yellow nut. Its brown skin is removed before being eaten, raw or cooked.

jeroan a general term for entrails. When ordering meat, one can ask whether a dish contains the fleshy parts of an animal (*daging*) or its internal organs (*jeroan*).

jeruk (jeruk limau) the general term for citrus fruits.

jeruk Bali pomelo or shaddock; it is a large, juicy grapefruit-like fruit with thick rind and pink or green flesh. Also called *jeruk besar* and *limau besar.*

jeruk besar see *jeruk* Bali.

jeruk bodong a type of citrus fruit with a thick, aromatic rind used to make candied peel. Also called *jeruk sukade.*

jeruk Garut tangerine-like fruit with easily peeled skin. Also called *jeruk keprok.*

jeruk keprok see *jeruk Garut.*

jeruk keriput grapefruit.

jeruk limo see *jeruk sambal.*

jeruk manis Indonesian orange, whose skin remains green after ripening. Also called *jeruk peres.*

jeruk nipis lime.

jeruk peres see *jeruk manis.*

jeruk purut Kaffir lime. Larger than our familiar lime, it has a prominant nipple at one end and warty skin; its juice is used as a souring agent. Of greater culinary importance than the fruit, the aromatic Kaffir lime leaves, or *daun jeruk purut,* are used as bay leaves, either fresh or dry, to add flavor to cooked foods.

jeruk sambal a marble-sized lime, which is sliced longitudinally and used as a condiment. Also called *jeruk limo* and *jeruk sundai.*

jeruk siam a type of tangerine with a hard-to-remove rind.

jeruk sitrun a lemon-like citrus fruit.

jeruk sukade see *jeruk bodong.*

jeruk sundai see *jeruk sambal.*

jintan caraway; also called *jemuju.* Cumin is also called *jintan.*

jintan hitam cumin; also see *jintan.*

jintan manis see *adas manis.*

jintan putih white cumin.

jumpul mullet.

juwet see *jamblang.*

kacang the general word for legumes—peanuts, beans and nuts. Note legumes are written two ways—the specific name is used alone, or in combination with the generic word *kacang.* For example, the specific name for soybean is *kedelei.* It is written as *kedelei* or *kacang kedelei.* Although both names are typically seen, only the specific name will be listed in this *Guide.* Some legumes always are referred to using both the generic and specific terms. Because of these variations in naming legumes, be sure to look under both the specific name and the entries under *kacang.*

kacang Arab a small, hard, black-skinned white bean, eaten as a snack.

kacang Bandung a small peanut; also called *kacang* Cina.

kacang belimbing peas; also called *kacang kapri* and *ercis*.

kacang Bogor a large, white peanut-like bean, which is roasted and eaten as a snack.

kacang Cina see *kacang* Bandung.

kacang goode the lentil-like pigeon pea.

kacang hijau (ijo) mung bean.

kacang Jawa lima bean.

kacang kapri see *kacang belimbing*.

kacang kedelei muda unripe soybeans still in the pod. Only the beans are eaten, boiled.

kacang merah kidney bean.

kacang mete the cashew nut. The nut grows at the tip of the "fruit" called *jambu mete* (see this *Guide*). It is enclosed in a green hull containing caustic compounds, which burn the mouth and lips if the nut is not roasted. Also called *gajus*.

kacang panjang a variety of green bean with pods up to three feet long. Older beans of this popular vegetable are cooked; young beans are eaten raw. Young leaves, or *lembayung,* are steamed and used in a salad of the same name (see *Menu Guide*).

kacang Shanghai see *canggai*.

kacang tanah peanut.

kacang tunggak black-eyed pea.

kakap snapper; also called *dorang* and *kakap hitam*.

kakap merah see *ikan merah*.

kakatua biru parrotfish.

kaki foot or leg.

kaki babi pig hocks.

kaki kambing goat or lamb's trotters.

kaki kodok frog's legs.

kaki lima "five-legged" food cart—a food vendor and his two-wheeled cart, which has a small-wheeled stand at the end to rest it.

kaldu broth, or soup stock.

kaliasem see *gowok*.

kalong see *keluang*.

kalui the *gurami* fish.

kambing goat or sheep; another word for sheep is *biri biri*.

kan a container for boiling tea.

kanari (kenari) the Javanese almond.

kangkung aquatic plant known as water spinach or swamp cabbage. Its wedge-shaped leaves taste like spinach and are primarily eaten cooked as a vegetable.

kanji see *pacar* Cina.

kaoliang sorghum.

kapri snowpea pods.

kapul (kapulaga) cardamom.

kapur sirih see *pinang*.

karak a Central Javanese rice cracker.

kare (kari) curry; another word for curry is *bagar*.

kaspe see *singkong*.

kastanye chestnut.

kates see *pepaya*.

kayu manis cinnamon.

kebuk a cylindrical utensil for making rice flour noodles.

kecap soy sauce.

kecap asin a thin, salty soy sauce. Some mixtures are somewhat spicy (hot).

kecap ikan a condiment made with soy sauce and fermented fish paste; also called *kecap petis*.

kecap manis sweet soy sauce; it is commonly thicker than the salty soy sauce, or *kecap asin*.

kecap petis see *kecap ikan*.

kecap sedang moderately salty soy sauce; less salty than *kecap asin*.

kecarum see *kemangi*.

kecil small; also see *makanan kecil*.

kecipir the winged or asparagus bean, which has four evenly spaced, ruffly extensions of the pod running along its length. It tastes a bit like asparagus.

kedai food stall; also called *lepau*.

kedai kopi cafe or coffee shop; it is a local meeting place for men only.

kedelei soybeans.

kedongdong the Otaheite (Tahiti) apple; it is a sour, green plum-like fruit with an apple-like taste. It is eaten raw or is stewed to make a sauce similar to applesauce.

keju cheese.

keju kacang peanut butter; also called *pindakas* and *selai kacang*.

kelabet fenugreek.

keladi see *talas*.

kelapa coconut.

Foods & Flavors Guide

kelapa muda a young coconut, whose white flesh is either soft or firm enough to be grated, but not hard. Soft coconut meat is eaten fresh, used in desserts or added to drinks along with the coconut water. Other names for young to semi-mature coconuts are *beluluk, kelapa sentengah tua,* and *kelongkong.*

kelapa muda santen coconut milk made from the meat of a young coconut.

kelapa parut grated coconut.

kelapa sawit a palm fruit used for making cooking oil. The orange-red, strawberry-sized fruits have oily orange pulp.

kelapa sentengah tua see *kelapa muda.*

kelapa tua a mature coconut with hard, white flesh covered with thin, brown skin that must be removed before grating.

keledek see *ubi jalar.*

kelengkeng the longan, a small, light-brown fruit from an evergreen tree. Its white, translucent flesh surrounds a single seed.

kelenjar perut sweetbreads.

kelinci see *arnab.*

kelongkong see *kelapa muda.*

keluak see *kluwek.*

keluang a large fruit-eating bat, called the flying fox, whose wings are considered a delicacy in certain parts of Indonesia. Also called *kalong* and *paniki.*

kemangi a variety of basil called English sweet basil, which has grayish leaves; also called *kecarum* and *ruku ruku.* Compare with *selasih.*

kemiri candlenut. It is a small, irregularly shaped beige nut used to flavor and thicken sauces and condiments, or *sambals.* It is ground together with fresh spices to make a paste. The nuts must be cooked before use because they are somewhat toxic when raw. Also called *kumbik.*

kenceng frying pan.

kencur lesser galangal, a brown, aromatic rhizome of the ginger family more pungent than the related spice called greater galangal, or laos. The rhizome's juicy, yellowish flesh is mixed with other fresh spices and ground into a paste. Often, both laos and ordinary ginger are included in the spice mixture, giving a heady ginger essence to a dish. Note that the juice stains skin and clothing.

kendil an earthenware cooking pot.

kenikir the edible leaves of the cosmos flower, used as a parsley-like garnish.

kental thick or strong.

kentang potato.

kepencong see *kluwek.*

kepiting crab.

kepundung see *menteng*.

kerang clam.

kerang kipas scallop.

kerapu grouper, sea perch or sea bass.

kerat a slice.

kerbau buffalo.

kering dried.

keripik see *kripik*.

kerneli vanilla; also called *panili*.

kersen cherry.

kertang a large grouper.

kerupuk see *krupuk*.

kesemek persimmon. This round, yellow or orange, tomato-like fruit is eaten raw or candied. Fruits to be candied are coated with limewater (*air kapur*) so they won't become mushy when boiled in sugar syrup. In the markets, these coated treated fruits are recognizable by the thin, white covering over much of their surface.

kesip seedless.

kesune see *bawang putih*.

ketan sticky (glutinous) white rice, typically used to make sweetmeats. Also called *beras ketan, beras pulut* and *pulut*.

ketan hitam long grain, sticky (glutinous) black rice. It is used to make a breakfast porridge (*bubur injin* or *bubur hitam*) eaten with palm sugar and coconut milk. It is also fermented to make a sweet wine (*brem*). The rice left behind after the wine is removed becomes a dessert (*tape*) and a drink (*es tape*). See *Menu Guide*. Also called *injin*.

ketar tart or sour.

ketela manis see *ubi jalar*.

ketela pohon the leaves of the cassava plant, used as a vegetable.

ketimbul the breadnut, or seeded breadfruit; it is a fruit with dark green skin studded with black spines. It resembles the seedless breadfruit, but its starchy, cream-colored flesh has many large seeds. The flesh is eaten fried, baked or boiled, but not raw. Also called *kluwih* and *timbul*.

ketimun cucumber. Also called *ketimun gantung*, or hanging cucumber. Other names are *lepang, mentimun* and *timun*.

ketimun gantung see *ketimun*.

ketimun guling a green, melon-sized cucumber, often with yellow or orange stripes, typically served in wedges.

ketola see *gambas*.

ketumbar coriander seed.

khamar wine or liquor.

kimpul see *talas.*

kismis see *anggur kering.*

kluwek the seed of the *kepayang* tree, which contains black, pasty material used as a spice. Fresh seeds contain hydrocyanic acid and must be detoxified with heat before use. This spice is a key ingredient in dishes such as *rawon* and *brongkos,* to which it imparts both a distinctive flavor and a dark color. Also spelled *keluak.* Another name for the seed is *kepencong.*

kluwih see *ketimbul.*

kodok frog.

kol cabbage; also called *kubis.*

kol kembang see *blumkol.*

kolak a sweet compote of starchy fruit cooked in coconut milk and palm sugar.

kolang kaling the fruits of the *aren* sugar palm, which are in three pods within the fibrous material of the small, green to purplish palm nuts. These pods must be shelled to obtain the white, fleshy fruits. They are boiled before being eaten, usually as sweetmeats in sugar syrup such as in the dish *wedang donga,* a ginger-flavored syrup containing peanuts, peanut-filled balls of sticky rice and *kolang kaling.* The shelled, boiled fruits, often colored pink, are stored in water until needed, and will be found this way in the markets. Note that the juice of the raw fruit can sting.

koma koma saffron.

komplit complete, "with all the trimmings," as opposed to *biasi,* or usual.

koni okra.

kopi coffee.

kopi celik cup of coffee.

kopi hitam black coffee (no cream).

kopi luak coffee made from ripe beans first ingested and excreted by the civet cat. Its superior quality is legendary, but it is no longer available in quantity for general consumption.

kopi susu coffee with milk.

kopi tanpa kafein decaffeinated coffee.

kopi tok unsweetened coffee.

kopi tubruk Turkish-style coffee.

kopyor a developmentally different coconut, whose meat remains soft and crumbly, and blended with its water. This prized coconut is used sweetened in a variety of desserts and drinks. It is more expensive than a regular coconut and to detect one requires much skill. Reliable fruit shops sell them with a money back-guarantee.

krecek see *krupuk jangat.*

kripik crisp, cracker-like snacks made of foods such as sweet potatoes, bananas and tempe. Also spelled *keripik.*

kroket croquette.

krokot see *gelang.*

krupuk crisp, cracker-like snacks made of several types of flour flavored primarily with fish (*krupuk ikan*) or shrimp (*krupuk udang*). During deep-frying, they expand to many times their original size. They also accompany meals, and as such, might be considered the "bread" of Indonesia, since there is no soft, leavened bread in the traditional Indonesian diet. A similar chip made from kernels of the *melinjo* nut are called *emping* (see this *Guide*). Also spelled *kerupuk.*

krupuk jangat (jangek) buffalo skin processed into a cracker snack; also called *krecek.*

krupuk Palembang crisp, cracker-like snacks flavored with *ikan belida,* a knifefish found in South Sumatra. To make this variety of *krupuk,* strands of dough are formed into nest-like shapes.

krupuk Sidoarjo large, crispy crackers named for the East Javanese city of Sidoarjo, from which *krupuk* is said to originate.

krupuk tempe crisp, cracker-like snacks made from tempe; also called *kripik.*

kuah broth, thin sauce or gravy.

kubis see *kol.*

kubis bunga see *blumkol.*

kue (kueh) the general word for cookie, cake or biscuit.

kue basah "moist" cakes—they have been boiled, steamed or deep-fried.

kue dadar a pancake-like dessert; also the name for a macaroon.

kue kering cookies, biscuits and "dry" cakes.

kue kue sweet foods. On menus, this word heads the dessert section.

kukusan a woven conical basket used to steam foods over boiling water.

kulat see *cendawan.*

kulit skin, peel or outer covering.

kulit padi rice chaff or bran. Also called *antah* and *bekatul.*

kulit pangsit wonton skins.

kumbik see *kemiri.*

kuning yellow.

kunyit (kunir) turmeric. The light brown rhizomes have bright orange flesh that is pounded into a paste along with other fresh spices. It is also used to color ceremonial rice and other foods yellow.

kupang a tiny shellfish found in East Java in the vicinity of Surabaya.

kurau threadfin breams; these fish are also called *senangin.*

labu the generic word for squash.

labu air a large, green calabash or bottle gourd, eaten as a vegetable.

labu hijau the wax gourd, which is candied or used in starchy fruit compotes called *kolak* (see *Menu Guide*).

labu kuning pumpkin or winter squash; also called *labu merah*.

labu merah see *labu kuning*.

labu siam the chayote, a pear-shaped, light-green squash with lengthwise furrows. Also called *waluh*.

lada pepper; also called *merica*.

lada hitam black pepper; also called *lada sulah* and *merica hitam*.

lada putih white pepper; also called *merica putih*.

lada sulah see *lada hitam*.

lada tumbuk ground pepper.

laksa fine, transparent noodles made of soybean flour; also called *su un*.

lamtoro see *pete* Cina.

laos greater galingal, a rhizome of the ginger family, which adds bitterness to a dish. It is ground into a paste with other spices, often including ordinary ginger and lesser galangal (see *kencur* this *Guide*). Also called *lengkuas*.

lapis layered.

latuh edible seaweed.

lawar a Balinese salad made from various finely chopped ingredients, traditionally mixed with uncooked blood, which reddens the preparation.

Lebaran the feast celebrating the end of the month-long fast of Puasa (Ramadan). Also called Idul Fitri in Arabic.

leci the fruit known as litchi nut. Ripe fruits are bright red with knobby, somewhat brittle skin. Their sweet, jelly-like pulp is translucent white and surrounds a single, large seed.

legian see *lesehan*.

legit sweet, stick or elastic.

lele a freshwater catfish.

lemak nabati vegetable oil.

lemak tulang see *sum sum*.

lembayung the leaves of the long bean (*kacang panjang*) plant and the name of a salad using them.

lemon cui a citrus fruit grown in North Sulawesi; it is a typical ingredient in the Minihasan sauce called *dabu dabu*.

lempok candied fruit, often made from the *durian*.

lengkeng see *rambutan lengkeng*.

lengkuas see *laos*.

lepang see *ketimun*.

lepau see *kedai.*

lesehan sitting on the floor and dining at low tables. Eating in this manner is common in Yogyakarta, Central Java. It is also called *legian* and *lincak.*

leunca a small, green fruit used in making condiments, or *sambals.*

lidah tongue.

limau besar see *jeruk* Bali.

limpa spleen.

lincak see *lesehan.*

lobak long, white daikon radish.

lobak Cina turnip.

lobak merah beet.

lobi lobi a small red fruit resembling a cherry, which is used in fruit salads.

lokio chives; also called *bawang kucai.*

lombok see *cabe.*

luding see *tenggiri.*

lulur beef tenderloin.

lumpia spring roll.

lunak tamarind pulp.

madu honey; also called *manisan lebah.*

magang overripe.

maisena cornstarch.

makan malam dinner.

makan pagi breakfast.

makan siang lunch.

makanan food.

makanan kecil snacks or appetizers. On menus, this word heads the appetizers section. Another word for snacks is *penganan,* or simply *kecil.*

mangga mango; also called *poh.*

mangga gadung see *mangga harum manis.*

mangga gedong small, round variety of mango with orange skin and sweet red flesh when ripe.

mangga golek large, elongated variety of mango with yellow-green skin and delicious, somewhat fibrous flesh.

mangga harum manis considered the tastiest of mangos. Probolinggo, East Java, is famous for them. Also called *mangga gadung.*

mangga kuini rather foul-smelling wild mango.

mangga manalagi medium-sized mango with delicious yellow flesh.

manggis mangosteen. About the size of a large lime, this fruit has thick purple rind and delicious, white, segmented flesh.

mangkuk cup or bowl.

manis sweet; with sugar (coffee).

manisan sweets or candy.

manisan buah candied fruit.

manisan lebah see *madu*.

manisan pala the candied flesh of the fruit whose seed is the nutmeg.

manting see *daun salam*.

markisah passionfruit, a green to yellowish fruit about the size of a large lemon. It contains many small seeds surrounded by delicious, juicy pulp. The small green varieties typically are used to make juice.

marus clotted blood used in cooking. Disk-shaped blocks of it can be seen stacked up in the markets. Also called *dideh*.

masakan Padang the hot (spicy) cuisine of the Minangkabau people of West Sumatra, which takes its name from the provincial capital, Padang.

masakan telur egg dishes; on menus, these words head the egg section. Also called *hidangan telur*.

matang ripe or cooked.

melinjo the red, olive-shaped fruit of the *melinjo* tree, whose kernels are used primarily to make crispy chips called *emping*. The ripe red peel is eaten fried. Unripe fruits, both the green skin and white kernel, and the leaves are eaten cooked in dishes such as *sayur asam* (see *Menu Guide*).

mem bontot see *bontotan*.

mendikai see *semangka*.

mentah unripe, raw, or uncooked food.

mentega butter.

menteng a small, round fruit with yellow-green skin covered with brown patches. The grape-like, white flesh is somewhat tart. Also called *kepundung*.

mentimun see *ketimun*.

merah red.

merah telur egg yolk.

merica see *lada*.

merica bulat peppercorns.

merica hitam see *lada hitam*.

merica putih see *lada putih*.

merunggai a small tree whose leaves are eaten as a vegetable.

mi (mie) egg noodles.

mihun see *bihun*.

miju miju lentils.

mindo leftovers from breakfast eaten with rice at lunch.

minuman a drink; on menus, it heads the beverage section.

minuman anggur wine.

minuman keras alcoholic drinks; on menus, it heads the alcoholic drinks section.

minuman tanpa alkohol nonalcoholic drinks.

minyak oil.

minyak goreng cooking oil.

minyak jagung corn oil.

minyak kacang tanah peanut oil.

minyak kelapa coconut oil; it is the solid, white "oil" from coconut meat.

minyak makan kelapa sawit oil from the palm fruit called *kelapa sawit*.

minyak wijen sesame oil.

minyak zaitun olive oil.

mua see *belut*.

mutiara see *sagu*.

nanas (nenas) pineapple. Also spelled *nenas*.

nanas seberang the large, sweet and juicy Sumatran pineapple.

nangka the jackfruit. It is an immense, oblong fruit, reaching weights of over 100 pounds, with thick yellow-green skin studded with hard projections. The fruit has little or no stem and grows directly from the bark of the tree. The light-yellow, segmented flesh tastes like sweet bananas, and surrounds large, oval seeds, which also are eaten, boiled. When sold in the markets, these immense fruits are hacked into manageable pieces or separated into individual pods with their enclosed seed. The ripe flesh of this popular fruit is eaten fresh or used in drinks such as *es campur* (see *Menu Guide*). Unripe fruit and young leaves of the tree are eaten as vegetables.

nangka belanda see *sirsak*.

nangka sabrang see *sirsak*.

nasi cooked rice.

nasi dan mi rice and noodles. On menus, these words head the "pasta" section.

nasi tambah a heaping bowlful of rice placed on the table in addition to the portion of rice already included with one's meal.

nasi tutu rice that is hulled by hand, often by beating it with stout wooden sticks.

nyambu see *jambu air*.

nyambu mente see *jambu mete*.

oncom a fermented paste made from the residue of peanuts after the oil has been extracted. It is steamed in banana leaves or fried.

opor a way of cooking meat or chicken in a "white" curry sauce—coconut milk and various spices, but no chili peppers.

otak brain.

oyong see *gambas.*

pa'piong (pakpiung) refers to food cooked in bamboo sections (see *bulu, this Guide*).

pacar Cina bits of hard, dried tapioca, sometimes colored, which are ingredients in desserts such as the East Javanese treat called *angsli* (see *Menu Guide*). Also called *kanji.*

padi the name for mature, harvested rice before it is polished or cooked.

paha meat from the upper leg of an animal.

pahit bitter; when applied to drinks, it means they are unsweetened.

pais see *pepes.*

pajak see *pasar.*

pakai with.

pakel a green fruit of the mango family, considered inferior in taste, and rarely eaten fresh.

pakis edible ferntops; also called *paku* and *sayur paku.*

paku see *pakis.*

pala nutmeg.

palai see *pepes.*

panas hot (not spicy) food.

pangek the West Sumatran (Minangkabau) style of cooking in which spices—typically ginger, greater galangal, lesser galangal (see *kencur*), shallots and small, hot chili peppers—are boiled in coconut milk until the oil comes to the surface. Then fish or chicken is added and simmered until done.

panggang baked or roasted over a fire.

pangsa a section or segment (of fruit); also called *ulas.*

paniki see *keluang.*

panili see *kerneli.*

pao biscuit.

pao timor bread.

pare (parai) bitter melon, gourd or cucumber; it is an oblong vegetable with bumpy skin. Green, immature melons are more edible because they have less fibrous flesh than yellow, ripe ones. Much of the vegetable is unusable;

after it is cored, only a narrow ring of flesh is left. It is used in raw vegetable dishes such as *lawar* (see *Menu Guide*).

pareh see *pedas*.

pari ray or skate.

paru lung.

parutan a grater.

pasar market; also called *pajak*.

pasar malam a night market.

pasar pagi a morning market.

pedas (pedes) hot (spicy) food; also called *pareh*.

pekan a weekly market.

penganan see *makanan kecil*.

penyu turtle.

pepaya papaya; also called *kates*.

pepes foods wrapped in a banana leaf and baked or steamed. Also caled *pais* and *palai*.

peret the fruit rat, which has a white-tipped tail. Its meat has a strong taste and odor.

pergulakan see *ulek ulek*.

periuk belanga a two-piece steamer made of clay.

perkedel (pergedel) a croquette or fritter of minced meat and corn or boiled potatoes. Also called *bregedel* and *frikadel*.

permen mint; also the general name for candy.

persik peach.

pete (petai) a tree-grown broad bean in foot-long pods so flat that the outline of individual beans within them is very prominent. The entire pod, sliced, is fried and eaten as a vegetable. Skinned beans—light green, flat and somewhat furrowed—are popular as a fried snack.

pete Cina a broad bean known as horse tamarind, which has shorter pods and flatter seeds than the *pete*. Also called *lamtoro*.

peterseli parsley.

petis a condiment made from jellied shrimp shells or fermented fish, which is used as a seasoning.

petola see *gambas*.

petulo a cake made of compacted, fine strands of a green-colored glutinous rice flour mixture that has been forced through an extruder. Small cubes of it are a key ingredient in the East Javanese dessert called *angsli* (see *Menu Guide*).

pinang the areca nut (commonly known as betel nut) from the areca palm tree. Another name for the nut is *jambe*. Slices of it are mixed with some lime (*kapur sirih*) and wrapped in a leaf (*sirih*) from a pepper-like plant to make a popular quid. The lime helps the stimulatory chemicals of the nut get into the bloodstream.

pindakas see *keju kacang*.

pindang a dish cooked with spices in water, not coconut milk, which often includes tamarind and soy sauce.

piring plate.

piring ceper a flat dish.

piring makan a shallow dish for eating rice.

pisang banana. In Bali, however, the generic name for banana is *biu*. Although the specific name is usually the same, e.g., *pisang mas* and *biu mas,* this *Guide* will have single entries, under *pisang*. Differences will be noted under the appropriate *biu* or *pisang* entry.

pisang Ambon large, green banana.

pisang batu stone banana. It contains many hard seeds.

pisang hijau long banana that remains green when ripe. Called *biu gading*, or ivory banana, in Bali.

pisang kayu wood banana; it is a thin, strong-flavored variety.

pisang kepok cooking banana.

pisang mas golden banana; it is a very small, sweet banana with thin skin.

pisang raja variety of long and fat, sweet banana with thick skin. It is often dipped in batter and fried.

pisang susu milk banana, a finger-length yellow banana with black spots.

pisang tandok plantain. It is typically dipped in batter and steamed.

pisang tuju variety of tiny banana.

pisau knife.

poh see *mangga*.

pokat see *alpokat*.

pondah hearts of palm.

porsi portion.

potongan a chop or slice of meat.

prem plum.

puarlaka cardamom.

Puasa a fast; the Indonesian month of fasting (Ramadan).

pucok nipah see *belut*.

pulut see *ketan*.

putih white.

putih telur egg white.

puyuh quail; also called *burung puyuh*.

rades radish.

ragi a fermentation agent such as yeast.

rambak beef or pork skin fried as chips.

rambat see *ubi jalar*.

rambutan a small, round fruit with red or orange-yellow rind covered with long, supple, hair-like projections. The fruits are easily peeled to obtain tart, translucent, white flesh like that of litchi nuts. The more flavorful varieties are lighter colored. Also called *aceh* and *buluan*.

rambutan lengkeng a variety of small, red-colored *rambutan*, which tastes like the fruit called *lengkeng*, or *kelengkeng*. It is not very juicy.

rambutan rabiah a yellow variety of *rambutan* considered the tastiest.

rebung bamboo shoot.

rebus see *godog*.

remah roti see *bubuk roti*.

remang see *belut*.

rembang a marble-sized, small, long-stemmed green vegetable, which is a standard ingredient of the salad *lalapan* (see *Menu Guide*).

remis mussel.

rempah a fritter, often containing coconut and beef (see *Menu Guide*).

rempah rempah any of several combinations of spices and roots, which are crushed to a paste and used to season curries and *sate*. Often these mixtures are sautéed briefly in oil to enhance and blend their flavors before other ingredients, commonly including coconut milk, are added.

rempela see *ampela*.

rempeyek crisp wafers or fritters made with peanuts; they are like savory peanut brittle.

rempeyek kacang see *gula kacang*.

restoran restaurant. In general, an eating place with WSesternized food will probably be called a *restoran*. More authentic cuisine is found in eateries called *rumah makan* and *warung*.

rica rica a fiery-hot chili paste containing red chili peppers, shallots, ginger and lime juice, which is used in cooking meat and fish dishes in North Sulawesi.

rom cream.

roti bread or bun.

roti bakar toast; also called *roti panggang*.

roti kabin salt crackers.

roti panggang see *roti bakar*.

roti tawar white bread.

ruku ruku see *kemangi*.

rumah makan a restaurant with authentic Indonesian preparations. A *restoran* tends to have more Westernized fare.

sagu sago, a starchy, low-protein food staple in the eastern islands of Indonesia. It is derived from the soft pith of the trunk of the sago palm. Water is added to pulverized pith to release its starch, which is then dried and eaten as a porridge. Droplets or "pearls," of sago, called *mutiara,* are made by sieving moistened sago, which has been colored pink or green. The droplets are then dried for use in desserts and drinks.

saguer see *tuak saguer.*

salai smoked.

salak the snake fruit, a palm fruit shaped like a pointed pear. Triangular, dark brown scales form its characteristic, snake-like skin. The multilobed, crisp flesh is light beige and somewhat tart. It is eaten fresh, or made into fruit compotes.

sambal a hot chili sauce or relish. It typically contains hot chili peppers, onions, garlic, sugar, salt and vinegar, and is used for cooking or as a table-top condiment. Several *sambals,* both cooked and uncooked, typically accompany a meal.

sambal goreng food fried in a spicy sauce; also the name for a condiment containing a paste of hot red peppers, water and salt (itself called *sambal ulek),* plus shallots, garlic, laos, lemon juice, fermented shrimp paste, tomato purée and coconut milk.

sambal ulek a paste of hot red peppers, water and salt, one of the simpler condiments, or *sambals,* available.

santen (santan) coconut milk.

santen encer see *santen kental.*

santen kental thick coconut milk. It is made by soaking grated fresh coconut meat in warm water for a few minutes and then squeezing the milk out of the gratings. Subsequent soakings and squeezings of the same gratings produce a thinner coconut milk call *santen encer.*

sapi cow.

sarden sardine. Also called *tembang* and *ikan kembung.*

sari buah fruit juice.

sate small chunks of marinated meat, poultry or seafood threaded on skewers and grilled over a fire. Dipping sauces typically accompany this dish. In Bali, the meat is frequently minced. A small ball of seasoned, minced meat is wrapped around a skewer much stouter than those used in most other regions of Indonesia. The skewers can be made of bamboo or even stalks of a ginger plant.

satru a type of cookie made with mung beans sweetened with palm sugar.

sauk ladle.

saur the meal eaten before dawn during Puasa (Ramadan).

saus sauce or gravy.

saus tomat tomato sauce or ketchup.

sawi mustard greens.

sawi hijau bok choi.

sawi hijau asinan broad-leaved mustard greens used as a vegetable or salted for use in pickled salads.

sawi putih Chinese cabbage.

sawo a small, ovoid fruit with reddish-brown skin and white, somewhat sweet, granular flesh. Also called *sawo kecik*.

sawo kecik see *sawo*.

sawo manila the sapodilla. It is a brown-skinned fruit, 2 to 4 inches in diameter, with a potato-like surface and sweet, yellow-brown granular pulp that tastes like honeyed pears. From 3 to 12 seeds are placed radially at the center. The sapodilla tree has a milky latex, or chicle, which was used in the manufacture of chewing gum. Fruits are eaten when bordering on overripe so that the levels of latex and tannin are palatable. Also called *ciku*.

sayap ayam chicken wing.

sayat slice.

sayur vegetable. It is also the name for a category of soup-like vegetable dishes—mixtures of vegetables partially cooked with spices, usually in a thin sauce with coconut milk.

sayur labu pumpkin.

sayur mayur the plural of vegetable. On menus, these words head the vegetable section.

sayur paku see *pakis*.

sayur sayuran a general term for vegetables; also simply called *sayuran*.

sedia items on the menu that are available or prepared.

sedikit gula a little sugar.

segar fresh.

sekar pala see *bunga pala*.

sekotang a ginger-flavored tea.

selada (sla, slada) lettuce or salad.

selada air watercress.

selai jam or jelly.

selai kacang see *keju kacang*.

selamatan a ceremony commemorating important occasions in life. It is richly interwoven with ritual foods such as the cone-shaped mound of rice stained yellow with turmeric (*nasi tumpeng* or *tumpeng selamatan*), which is served on a large circular platter surrounded by a number of other dishes.

selasih a variety of basil with purplish stems. Its crushed leaves smell somewhat like licorice. The seeds are used in desserts and certain drinks such as *es selasih* (see *Menu Guide*). Also spelled *telasih*. Another word for this plant is *indring*.

selederi celery.

semangka watermelon. There are two common types—a pink-fleshed variety with green skin and a yellow-fleshed variety with striped green skin. Also available are small watermelons called *mendikai,* or *tembikai.*

semur a dish of meat stewed with soy sauce and aromatic spices such as nutmeg, cloves and pepper.

senangin see *kurau.*

sendok spoon.

sendok makan tablespoon.

sendok teh teaspoon.

sepat sour, or astringent.

sepek bacon.

serbet napkin.

sere see *trasi.*

sereh lemon grass; it is used primarily fresh. The less fibrous inner core at the bulb end is pounded into a paste.

setrop see *stroop.*

shimeji see *jamur tiram.*

singgang a West Sumatran (Minangkabau) method of cooking meat, especially chicken. The dressed bird is cut open and the two, almost separated halves spread apart (spread-eagled). It is cooked in spices and coconut milk (see *singgang ayam, Menu Guide*).

singkong manioc (cassava), a long, brown tuber rich in starch. The bitter variety is poisonous when raw. The hydrogen cyanide, or prussic acid, present in these tubers must be removed by extensive washing and cooking before the tubers become edible. Juice extracted from the pulp is the source of tapioca and flour is made from the pulp. Prussic acid in the sweet variety of cassava occurs primarily in the skin, which is removed by peeling. These tubers require less demanding preparative steps before they are safe to eat. Also called *kaspe* and *ubi kayu.*

sirih the leaf of a plant related to pepper. It is used as a wrapper for the areca nut (betel nut) and lime enjoyed by betel nut chewers. A mild euphoric state is produced by chewing this quid.

sirsak the soursop. It is a large, asymmetrically heart-shaped fruit with dark-green skin bearing many short soft projections. The segmented white pulp is mildly acidic and has an aroma of pineapple. Juice is made from the pulp; sweeter fruits are eaten fresh. Avoid the toxic seeds. Also called *nangka belanda, nangka sabrang* and *durian belanda.*

sitrun citron.

siwalan the nut from the palmyra palm. Its meat is used in desserts.

sop (sup) a soup-like dish of mixed vegetables and meat or chicken usually in a clear, mildly seasoned broth. Compare with *soto* (this *Guide*). On menus, this word heads the section of soup-like dishes.

sosis sausage.

soto soup-like dish of mixed vegetables and meat in a rich, seasoned broth. Compare with *sop* (this *Guide*). It is spelled *coto* in some areas.

sotong cuttlefish.

stroop a syrup available bottled in many flavors. It is used for cordials or added to coconut water to make soft drinks. Also spelled *setrop.*

su un see *laksa.*

sukun the breadfruit. The skin of this dark green fruit has a pattern of 4- to 6-sided facets, often with tiny spines in the center. Its starchy, cream-colored flesh is seedless, unlike the similar looking breadnut, or seeded breadfruit. The flesh is eaten fried, baked or boiled, but not raw.

sumsum (sungsum) bone marrow. Also called *lemak tulang.*

susu milk.

susu segar fresh milk.

tabia see *cabe.*

tabia gede a large chili pepper.

tahu tofu, a soft curd made from soybean milk, available in small cakes.

tahu kuning soybean curd that has been colored on the surface with yellow food coloring.

tahua soft soybean milk curd.

takjil sweetmeats eaten after breaking a fast.

talas taro, a starchy, edible root. The large leaves of the plant are used as a green vegetable or as an impromptu umbrella. Also called *keladi* and *kimpul.*

tambahan a bonus of extra produce given by vendors to their regular customers at the markets.

tambul dessert; it is also the name for snacks eaten with beverages.

tanpa see *tidak.*

tape (tapai) cooked cassava or black sticky rice that has been fermented with a mold to produce a slightly alcoholic product tasting like wine. It is eaten as a "cake" without further embellishment or is served with a bit of shaved ice, sometimes topped with syrup (see *tape, Menu Guide*).

tauco a condiment made with fermented yellow or black soybeans, crushed to a paste.

tauge bean sprouts; also called *tokolan*.

teh tea.

teh botol bottled or packaged tea.

teh es iced tea.

teh pahit unsweetened tea.

teh susu tea with milk.

telasih see *selasih*.

telur (telor) egg.

telur ceplok a fried egg.

telur godog a boiled egg.

telur kocokan a scrambled egg.

telur setengah matang a soft-boiled egg.

telur mata sapi a fried egg, sunny side up.

telur pindang an egg boiled in water flavored with tamarind, chili peppers, shallots, guava leaves and other seasonings.

telur puyuh a quail egg; it is a small, spotted egg, sometimes artfully arranged in boxes in the markets. Quail eggs are commonly hard boiled, stained black by steeping in a concoction made with guava leaves, and served skewered on tiny sticks, end to end, looking a lot like black olives.

tembang see *sarden*.

tembikai see *semangka*.

tempe (tempeh) cooked, whole soybeans that have been mixed with a mold and fermented in banana leaves for a few days. The mold fills the spaces between beans, making a compact, protein-rich cake, and helps break down soybean components that are otherwise indigestible. Typically it is sliced and fried.

tenggiri Spanish or king mackerel. Also called *luding*.

tengguli see *ceng*.

tepung flour.

tepung beras rice flour.

tepung gula confectioners' sugar.

tepung hoen kwe see *tepung kacang hijau*.

tepung kacang hijau mung bean flour. Also called *tepung hoen kwe*, or simply *hoen kwe*.

tepung pulut sticky (glutinous) white rice flour. It is used to make a chewy dough for a variety of sweetmeats, including the taffy-like confection called *dodol* (see *Menu Guide*).

tepung singkong manioc (cassava) flour.

tepung terigu wheat flour.

terasi see *trasi.*

terigu wheat.

terong eggplant.

terong lalap small, round eggplant, either green, white or purple, which is a common ingredient of the salad called *lalap* (see *Menu Guide*).

terubok shad; its roe is prized.

terwelu see *arnab.*

tesi teaspoon.

tidak without; *tanpa* also means "without."

tidak mau gula without sugar.

tidak pakai daging without meat.

tim steamed foods.

timbul see *ketimbul.*

timun see *ketimun.*

tino ransat pork dishes in North Sulawesi flavored with two forms of fresh herbs and roots—chopped and mashed—mixed together with fresh pork blood. Dishes called *woku* have a similar style of seasoning, but they are not limited to pork, and do not contain pork blood.

tiram oyster.

tokolan see *tauge.*

tomat tomato.

tomat belando a small, pink, oval fruit used for juice.

tongcai salted greens.

tongkol see *cakalang.*

tongseng a dish prepared with cabbage and usually lamb.

trasi fermented shrimp paste; also spelled *terasi*. Another word for this paste is *sere.*

tripang see *gamat.*

tuak yeasty, beer-like alcoholic drink or toddy made by fermenting sticky (glutinous) rice or the juice (sap) of unopened flowers from various types of palm trees, especially the coconut palm. Fresh juice is called *tuak manis,* or sweet *tuak*. It is very low in alcohol because the fermentation process has hardly begun. *Tuak wayah,* or old *tuak,* is at most a few days old and is preferred over the juice freshly removed from the tree. After a few days, the solution sours. The strong brandy-like drink called *arak* is made by distilling *tuak* (see *arak,* this *Guide*).

tuak saguer yeasty beer-like drink made in North Sulawesi from the sago palm.

tumis sauté or stir-fry.

tumpeng selamatan see *selamatan*.

tunjang jellied meat from trotters.

tusuk skewer.

ubi general term for edible tuber; it also can mean sweet potato.

ubi jalar sweet potato, or yam; it is also called *keledek, ketela manis, rambat* and simply *ubi*.

ubi kayu see *singkong*.

udang shrimp.

udang barong spiny lobster.

udang besar lobster.

udang galah huge river shrimp.

udang kering dried shrimp.

udang pancet tiger prawn.

ulas see *pangsa*.

ulek ulek clay pestle, used with a clay mortar called a *cobek,* to grind or crush fresh spices into a paste. Also called *pergulakan*.

unggas poultry.

usus see *isi perut*.

wajan wok-like cast-iron cooking pan with a rounded bottom.

waluh see *labu siam*.

warung an unpretentious outdoor food stall with long communal tables and benches serving authentic Indonesian homestyle cooking. Awnings provide a sun shield, some privacy and a prominent place to print the main menu items for all to see.

wijen sesame seed.

woku cooking method used in Sulawesi. Preparations are seasoned with fresh herbs and roots, and cooked in pots, in green bamboo sections or wrapped in palm leaves. Typically, some of the seasonings are crushed to a paste; others are chopped. These two mixtures are blended together, sautéed and then rubbed onto fish, pork or chicken before cooking.

wortel carrot.

zaitun olive.

Bibliography

Allen, Betty Molesworth. *Malayan Fruits: An Introduction to the Cultivated Species.* Singapore: Eastern Universities Press, Ltd, 1965.

Armawa, Sarita, editor. *Paon Bali: A Guide to the Balinese Kitchen.* Sanur, Bali, Indonesia: Bali Hyatt, 1983.

Boxer, C.R. *The Dutch Seaborne Empire: 1600–1800.* London: Hutchinson & Co Ltd, 1965.

Brierley, Joanna Hall. *Spices: The Story of Indonesia's Spice Trade.* Kuala Lumpur: Oxford University Press, 1994.

Brissenden, Rosemary. *South East Asian Food: Indonesia, Malaysia and Thailand.* Baltimore, Maryland: Penguin Books, Inc., 1972.

Chatterji, B.R. *History of Indonesia: Early and Medieval.* Meerut, India: Meenakshi Prakashan, 1963.

Cobley, Leslie S. *An Introduction to the Botany of Tropical Crops.* London: Longmans, Green and Co., Ltd, 1965.

Dalton, Bill. *Indonesian Handbook,* 5th edition. Chico, California: Moon Publications Inc., 1991.

Davidson, Alan. *Seafood: A Connoisseur's Guide and Cookbook.* New York: Simon and Schuster, 1989.

DeWit Antoinette and Anita Borghese. *The Complete Book of Indonesian Cooking.* Indianapolis, Indiana: The Bobbs-Merrill Company, Inc., 1973.

Eiseman, Fred B., Jr. *Bali: Sejaka and Niskala,* volume I. Scottsdale, Arizona: Fred B. Eiseman, Jr., 1985.

Eiseman, Fred B., Jr. *Bali: Sejaka and Niskala,* volume II. Scottsdale, Arizona: Fred B. Eiseman, Jr., 1986.

Fell, R.T. *Early Maps of South-East Asia,* 2nd edition. Singapore: Oxford University Press, 1991.

Hyman, Gwenda L. *Cuisines of Southeast Asia: A Culinary Journey Through Thailand, Myanmar, Laos, Vietnam, Malaysia, Singapore, Indonesia and the Philippines.* New York: John Wiley & Sons, Inc., 1993.

Johns, Yohanni. *Dishes from Indonesia*. Philadelphia, Pennsylvania: Chilton Book Company, 1971.

Marks, Copeland. *The Exotic Kitchens of Indonesia: Recipes from the Outer Islands*. New York: M. Evans and Company, Inc., 1989.

Marks, Copeland and Mintari Soeharjo. *The Indonesian Kitchen*. New York: Atheneum, 1981.

Masefield, John, editor. *Dampier's Voyages*. New York: E.P. Dutton & Co., 1906.

Masselman, George. *The Cradle of Colonialism*. New Haven, Connecticut: Yale University Press, 1993.

Morison, Samuel Eliot. *The European Discovery of America: The Southern Voyages 1492–1616*. New York: Oxford University Press, 1974.

Norman, Jill. *The Complete Book of Spices*. New York: Viking, 1991.

Ochse, J.J. *Vegetables of the Dutch East Indies*. Amsterdam: A. Asher & Co. B.V., 1977.

Ortiz, Elisabeth Lambert. *The Encyclopedia of Herbs, Spices and Flavourings: A Cook's Compendium*. New York: Dorling Kindersley, Inc., 1992.

Owen, Sri. *Indonesian Food and Cookery*. Jakarta, Indonesia: Gaya Baru, 1984.

Owen, Sri. *Indonesian Regional Cooking*. New York: St. Martin's Press, 1995.

Passmore, Jacki. *The Encyclopedia of Asian Food and Cooking*. New York: Hearst Books, 1991.

Piper, Jacqueline M. *Fruits of South-East Asia: Facts and Folklore*. Singapore: Oxford University Press, 1989.

Rosengarten, Frederic, Jr. *The Book of Spices*. Wynnewood, Pennsylvania: Livingston Publishing Company, 1969.

Samuel-Hool, Leonie. *To All My Grandchildren: Lessons in Indonesian Cooking*. Berkeley, California: Liplop Press, 1981.

Sek-Hiang, Lie. *Indonesian Cookery*. New York: Bonanza Books, 1963.

Skrobanek, Detlef, Suzanne Charlé and Gerald Gay. *The New Art of Indonesian Cooking*. Singapore: Times Editions, 1988.

Spruyt, J. and J.B. Robertson. *History of Indonesia: The Timeless Islands*. South Melbourne, Australia: The Macmillan Company of Australia Pty Ltd, 1973.

Suleiman, Satyawati. *Concise Ancient History of Indonesia*. Jakarta: The Archaeological Foundation, 1974.

Turner, Peter, Brendan Delahunty, Paul Greenway, James Lyon, Chris McAsey and David Willett. *Indonesia: A Lonely Planet Travel Survival Kit,* 4th edition. Victoria, Australia: Lonely Planet Publications, 1995.

Vlekke, Bernard H.M. *Nusantara: A History of the East Indian Archipelago*. New York: Arno Press, 1977.

Waugh, Teresa, translator. *The Travels of Marco Polo*. London: Sidgwick & Jackson, 1984.

Index

design   Ekeby
cover design   Susan P. Chwae
color separations   Widen Enterprises
printing   Thomson-Shore, Inc.

typefaces   Garamond Simoncini and Helvetica Black
paper   60 lb Joy White

ORDER FORM

Use this form to order additional copies.

Please send me:

_____ copies of *Eat Smart in Indonesia: How to Decipher the Menu, Know the Market Foods and Embark on a Tasting Adventure* @ $12.95 each.

Please add $2.00 postage and handling for one book, 50¢ for each additional book. Wisconsin residents add 5% sales tax.

☐ check enclosed for $ _____

☐ please charge my: ☐ MasterCard   ☐ VISA

Card # _____ Exp. Date: _____

_____
Signature

Name: _____

Address: _____

City: _____ State: ____ Zip: _____

Comments:

Your suggestions will be helpful for future editions of the book.

_____

_____

_____

_____

_____

Ginkgo Press, Inc.
P. O. Box 5346
Madison, Wisconsin 53705
Tel: 608-233-5488 Fax: 608-233-0053
http://www.ginkgopress.com